MOMMY, CAN BOYS ALSO BE DOCTORS?

MOMMY, CAN BOYS ALSO BE DOCTORS?

A MESSAGE TO YOUNG SCIENTISTS AND OTHER HUMANS

MARLENE BELFORT, PhD

COPYRIGHT © 2025 MARLENE BELFORT
All rights reserved.

MOMMY, CAN BOYS ALSO BE DOCTORS?
A Message to Young Scientists and Other Humans

FIRST EDITION

ISBN   978-1-5445-4815-9 *Hardcover*
           978-1-5445-4813-5 *Paperback*
           978-1-5445-4814-2 *Ebook*

*This book is dedicated to Georges for making me what I became;
to Dave, Gabi, and Yona for fulfilling my dreams;
and to the women in my life for sustaining me from the start.*

CONTENTS

Foreword 9
Preface 13

PART ONE: CHILD OF IMMIGRANTS
1. Raised in Three Parallel Universes 23
2. A Crash Course in Tragedy and Resilience 33
3. A Wider World—and a New Family Member 39
4. Falling in Love *and* Falling in Love with Science 45
5. Finding One's Place in the World 55

PART TWO: MOTHER AND SCIENTIST
6. A Baby, and a Career 67
7. A Supportive Environment for Working Women—Imagine That! 75
8. A Struggle and the Big Breakthrough 83
9. The Curse and the Blessing of the Successful Female Scientist 91
10. Helping Others See the Win-Win 105

PART THREE: RESILIENCE IN SICKNESS AND IN HEALTH
11. Resilience for Scientists 119
12. Depression Is a Different Story 123
13. The Door to Depression Remains Ajar 131
14. Each Loss Is an Opportunity 139

PART FOUR: PARTNERSHIPS IN SCIENCE AND IN LIFE

15. Scientific Collaborations Are Wonderful but Fraught 147
16. A Couple That Does Science Together... 153
17. Convergence Creole 161
18. Women Supporting Women 167
19. Building Diverse Communities 177

PART FIVE: THE FOURTH QUARTER

20. Looking Back at Life in Basic Research—the Privilege, the Value.... 187
21. Major Moves 197
22. The One Last Bias 205
23. Intergenerational Interactions 209
24. Passing the Baton 221

Afterword 227
Acknowledgments 231
About the Author 235

FOREWORD

—PAUL GRONDAHL
OPALKA ENDOWED DIRECTOR, NYS WRITERS INSTITUTE AT THE
UNIVERSITY AT ALBANY
OCTOBER 26, 2024

It would be understandable to consider Marlene Belfort solely for her substantial accomplishments and recognitions as a molecular biologist and research scientist, whose work focuses on basic science and applications in biotechnology and medicine. She has reached the pinnacle of her profession, as evidenced by her selection as a fellow of the American Academy of Arts and Sciences, her admission to the United States National Academy of Sciences, and the millions of dollars in research grants from the National Institutes of Health that she brought to the Belfort Lab at the prestigious RNA Institute at the University at Albany, where she is a distinguished professor.

That would be an illustrious scientific career by any measure. Belfort has been my colleague for the past eight years at UAlbany, where she was awarded the university's highest honor, the Academic Citizen Laureate Award, in 2019. I have observed her influence and legacy in the dozens of PhD and post-doctoral fellows she has mentored and her commitment as an advocate for the underrepresented and for promoting careers of women in science.

These scientific and professional accolades tell only a part of the story, however, as we learn in her revealing new book, *Mommy, Can Boys Also Be Doctors? A Message to Young Scientists and Other Humans.* Beginning with the provocative title, Belfort is not content to sugarcoat the truth or simply accept the status quo. She is a deeply intellectual and fiercely independent thinker, as well as a skillful prose stylist and storyteller. In fact, her singular approach has created a book that defies categorization. It is a hybrid narrative, melding elements of personal memoir with scholarly analysis, and giving an overarching theme that offers a complicated message to young, aspiring scientists. There is nothing tentative about Belfort's writing. She pushes back hard against the patriarchy of scientific research and she is open and honest about the many setbacks and obstacles she faced and worked hard to overcome.

At its heart, this is a love story about Marlene and Georges Belfort, who met as teenagers on a beach in Cape Town, South Africa, and whose marriage has spanned six decades. Both are esteemed research scientists, and their academic appointments have taken them from South Africa to Israel, California to New York, and beyond. The couple has weathered many storms together, which Belfort does not flinch from recounting. She suffered severe late-onset depression in her fifties and seventies that required lengthy hospitalizations and shock therapy. She dedicates her book to her beloved Georges, "for making me what I became," she writes. They are inseparable.

Belfort's story unfolds in many layers and is at times heartbreaking, beginning with her father's suicide, under mysterious circumstances, when she was thirteen. The daughter of German Jewish immigrants who settled in Cape Town, South Africa, her strong-willed mother—left a single parent with limited formal education—taught her daughter about resilience. Marlene and Georges studied at the University of Cape Town during the Apartheid era, and the couple did what they could to protest and resist the racist regime, but eventually both left South Africa as a statement against Apartheid's inhumanity.

Belfort's book is an extended meditation on and an impassioned conversation about the role of women in science; the unsolvable balance of personal and professional lives; the upsides and downsides of striving for high-level scientific and academic achievement; and what it means to live a good life.

I especially enjoyed the epigraphs at the start of each section, quotations from acclaimed authors and esteemed historical figures. It is a pleasure for me to see Marlene and Georges at many of our literary events presented by the New York State Writers Institute at UAlbany. They often join me and our literary guests for dinner, where they are lively conversationalists, witty and erudite, truly citizens of the world.

Belfort's book will make you laugh and cry, and it will leave you with lingering questions that have no easy answers. This hybrid of memoir and message is a glorious journey brimming with all the joy and heartache of the human condition. It carries a theme that a career in science and academia often is not linear. This book is a case study for young, aspiring scientists; a love letter to Georges; and a hosanna to the couple's three sons, three daughters-in-law, and seven grandchildren. Read it, as I did, with wonder and gratitude.

PREFACE

A MESSAGE TO THE NEXT GENERATION

"Everything that you think is solid is actually fleeting and ephemeral. The only thing that is quasi-permanent would be a book or work of art or photographs or something. Anything you create that transcends time is in some ways more real than the actual reality of your life."
—Joyce Carol Oates

At this stage of my life and career, approaching age eighty, I have the good fortune of still possessing the vitality, wherewithal, and good health to continue to engage productively with both my scientific work (though I'm no longer doing lab research) and my wonderful family. And having lived a long and full life—as a child of immigrants and shy schoolgirl who lost her father to suicide, then an immigrant herself as well as a mother, mentor, scientist, wife, friend, and sometimes adversary—I have a few messages for the next generation.

First, there's a message for young scientists, many of whom assume that a successful career starts with a clear vision when they graduate college and progresses on a linear trajectory until eventually they succeed and are recognized for their work. Wrong! Many careers proceed in fits and starts, with interruptions, sidetracks, and delays. There can be a discomfiting sense of just muddling through, which I actually consider an important process. It's essential to be at ease with uncertainty and sit with it long enough that the path forward emerges. One needs to learn to embrace the ambiguity as preparation for the next step. Certainly, there was nothing linear about my own scientific journey, which needed to adjust to accommodate all sorts of other circumstances, including my own lack of preparation and direction, as well as mothering, moving across oceans and continents, and battling serious illness.

But I'm getting ahead of myself. Before I tell those tales, I want to introduce my second message, this time for those considering parenthood. This may sound simplistic, but I say, "If it's in your heart to do it, do it!" I have written extensively—though mostly in scientific journals until now—on the mutually reinforcing roles of parenthood and a professional life, and yes, that message will be conveyed again in this book. In my own case, I have had extraordinary support in both roles from my husband, Georges Belfort, and there's no doubt in my mind that I'm a better scientist because I'm a happy mom and a better mom because I'm a distracted scientist. But this perspective is far from the norm, and it's still all too easy to succumb to negativity, mainstream thinking, and societal pressure. Even if you just honestly think you'll be a better professional if you're all-in at your job or a better parent if you don't work outside the home, the question deserves a closer look. You may be wrong again.

I have a third message for young parents who feel guilty because they think they're not devoting enough time and energy to their children or they're dragging their children around the world from job to job. I'm convinced that benign and loving neglect can foster independence in children and an itinerant lifestyle can in fact forge family bonds that last a lifetime. (Yes, I am reclaiming neglect as an unlikely virtue, as long as it's a sort of casual negligence balanced by kindness, devotion, and love!) There's no getting around the fact that we, women especially, often carry enormous angst as we attempt to juggle our personal lives with our professional ambitions. No one is immune to this burden altogether or all the time. But through the years, I've come to the happy realization that the very activities we catastrophize over and fear will damage our children often do the opposite, building their resilience, connections, and connectedness.

Resilience has been key for me throughout my life, as I've seen plenty of tragedy as well as triumph. I was born in Cape Town, South Africa, to German Jewish immigrant parents, and at thirteen, I lost my father to suicide. This cataclysmic event strengthened the already tight bond I had with my mother, who was my role model, despite her not having graduated high school. But I became disillusioned with a future under the Apartheid regime. There was no way to make a difference *and* stay out of jail. Protesting the government's oppressive racial policies was punishable by arrest and often imprisonment. So, after graduating college with a degree in science, I decided to go abroad to explore while visiting family and friends in Israel, England, and the US. The US leg of the trip was to visit a childhood sweetheart, Georges, who would become my husband. Meanwhile, I needed to work to afford my travels, so I spent time as a lab tech at the Weizmann Institute in Israel and a chambermaid in London, England. These experiences were formative but led to more questions. I knew I needed to do something worthwhile with my life. But what? And where?

After visiting Georges in California, I was pulled in opposite directions that were ten thousand miles apart: on one side, my mother and friends in Cape Town; on the other, Georges and a scientific future in California. After "being with" the dilemma, as I like to put it, and with Georges, traveling from Disneyland in Southern California to Mammoth Lakes in the north, talking about science and politics and just about everything else, it became clear to me I was deeply in love and needed to marry this man. So, that is what I did, and after our wedding, I returned to California for graduate school.

These events marked the beginning of a domestic and professional collaboration that has stood not just the test of time but many other tests as well. There have been highs and lows, periods of health and illness. And though it can seem like a blink of an eye, amazingly, our partnership has endured for more than half a century—during which time we somehow wound up with many scientific publications, three sons, three daughters-in-law, and seven wonderful grandchildren.

How did I manage, through it all, to navigate the complicated web of personal and professional impulses and obligations? Not without struggle; that's for sure. It was often difficult and confusing. But ultimately, I found space to live with my confusion, battle against sexist discrimination, follow my passions, and strive for not just excellence in science but also some sort of equilibrium between my home and the workplace. For four years, we lived in Israel, where our second and third sons were born while I was a post-doc. The supportive environment enjoyed by women there allowed most moms to work outside the home and greatly enabled my ability to combine my scientific career with parenting.

But despite my successes as a scientist and a mom, my life's journey has also been punctuated by sudden and profound waves of agony. One was as a child, of course, when I lost my dad. But I have also suffered two lengthy bouts of major, late-onset depression: one in my fifties; the other in my seventies. Both times, I was heavily medicated, hospitalized, and treated with shock therapy, also known as ECT (electroconvulsive therapy), an approach that has long been controversial and many don't even realize is still in use. I struggled through these depressive episodes, which lasted several years each, and had to claw my way back after recovery.

Again, resilience was key. But I'm not writing a "How to Be Resilient" book. And I know that doling out advice can become a dodgy and difficult affair. What's right for one is wrong for another. Moreover, what's universally accepted tends to make for mundane recommendations. In my trade as a molecular biologist, for example, everyone already knows the imperative to "publish or perish" is very real; I would rightly get eye rolls if I took to bloviating on something so obvious. So, I'm going to steer clear, for the most part, of giving advice per se. Rather, my aim is to extract meaningful principles from a life that has followed some passions and sacrificed others. It's not about "having it all," as the cliché goes; it's about what's most important for the moment *and* the duration.

When I give scientific seminars, they are usually well received, but when I give talks on how we negotiate the personal and professional aspects of our lives (and specifically what's called "work–life integration"), I notice my words resonate with the audience in a different way. I see in their faces that I'm hitting at the core of their ambivalence.

It tells me we must keep having these conversations.

In fact, it's a big part of what inspired me to write this book. We need to talk more about all these important matters: ambivalence, uncertainty, low morale, nonlinear paths to success, overcoming adversity, and mustering the courage to change direction.

Above all, we need to talk about the power and potential for shaping our worlds—those of our homes and workplaces but also our institutions and governing bodies—to better support the fundamental human endeavor of pursuing a happy, meaningful life in *all* its complex layers.

PART ONE

CHILD OF IMMIGRANTS

> *"What drew me to my craft was the desire to force the two worlds I occupied to mingle on the page as I was not brave enough, or mature enough, to allow in life."*
>
> —Jhumpa Lahiri

Growing up in Cape Town, South Africa, in the mid-1900s was like inhabiting three parallel universes.

First was the universe of my immigrant family, the Sterns, where German was our language at home since my Oma (grandmother) spoke little English. All our family friends were German Jewish refugees who had escaped the Nazis. Like many of these friends, my parents were retail clothes merchants. Other German Jewish families also sold cars, furniture, or rugs.

My school friends occupied my second universe. They all spoke English as a first language, and many of their fathers were professionals: doctors, lawyers, accountants, and the like. One was even the mayor of Cape Town. None of their mothers worked, not even in their homes, which were staffed by "servants," leaving the moms free to drive their children to and from school. My mom needed to work to help support our family, meaning I had to walk to school or take the bus. Though it makes me wince to say it now, I admired my school friends' families, with their fancy jobs and higher education, and felt ashamed of my own.

My third universe was made up of Africans and "Coloreds" (people of mixed race). These were the folks who worked in our homes and businesses but were completely excluded from the civic, political, and social lives of the privileged whites. They spoke African languages, like Xhosa and Zulu, or Afrikaans, a bastardized form of Dutch, which we all had to learn in school. "Oma," for example, means "grandmother" in Afrikaans but is a term commonly used by all South Africans, my own family included. (It also happens to be the same word in German, only pronounced a little differently.)

This was the Apartheid era of racial segregation: Whites were the privileged class while urban "Blacks" and "Coloreds" lived in slums or shantytowns or as servants in the homes of the "Europeans" (the standard name for whites). "Apartheid," Afrikaans for "apartness or separateness," was strictly enforced in South Africa between 1948 and 1991, where political and economic discrimination against non-whites, who were the majority, was enshrined in the law. There were separate entrances to buildings for whites and non-whites as well as "Whites Only" signs on park benches and at the entrances to movie theaters, beaches, and buses. Schools were segregated, and people of color, as we'd say nowadays, were essentially excluded from urban universities. The white minority was made up of mostly Afrikaners, who are descendants of the Dutch settlers of the mid-seventeenth century, and the British, who took control in the mid-nineteenth century. The Afrikaners, mainly farmers, were the architects of Apartheid and extraordinarily racist, whereas those of British descent were mainly urban liberals. Apartheid was so extreme that it produced and enforced the Immorality Act, which forbade interracial sexual relationships. This act is the basis of the title of Trevor Noah's book *Born a Crime*, Noah being the son of a Black African mother and white Swiss father.[1]

That's my abbreviated, CliffsNotes version of Apartheid-era South Africa and the acutely segregated world in which I grew up. Segregated by law, not just custom, and enforced through state power and violence. As I wrote at the top of this section, it was like living in separate universes. But I was drawn to all those universes and deeply influenced by figures in my early life from outside my immediate family and community. One might say that instead of occupying two worlds, as Lahiri did (see opening quote), I occupied three: my immigrant family, my white South African friends, and the non-white people who worked in our homes and businesses and whom I spent countless hours with as a kid. In my college years, we socialized across the color barrier a bit, particularly with Colored musicians, who played at our dance parties and snuck in a quick dance and smooch when

---

[1] Trevor Noah, *Born a Crime: Stories from a South African Childhood* (One World, 2016).

no one was looking. Of course, this was strictly against the law. All three of these worlds contributed to my adult persona and made me who I am today.

I cherished my three worlds but also felt somewhat apart from each of them, even from the German Jewish community my family belonged to. Feeling like an outsider was a constant theme in those early years, and I think that comes very much from my immigrant upbringing. It was something I would attempt to overcome throughout my life. But maybe, we never fully shed that feeling of otherness? And in my case, not only was I a child of immigrants, I was also the girl whose dad went missing and then was found dead in an apparent suicide.

It was a lot to try to overcome. The emotional residue of that tragedy sticks with me to this day. At the time, I was able to partly ease the terrible burden of loss, or at least escape it for a while, by traveling the world on my first big trip away from Cape Town. But when I returned, new challenges emerged. For starters, I had to accept my beloved mother's new marriage, to an orthodox rabbi no less. I wanted her to have a new partner, but admittedly, I held some serious reservations about this particular relationship. By this point, I was already in love with science and suspicious of religious fervor in general. Naturally, I needed a moment to get used to the idea of an orthodox rabbi becoming my mom's new mate!

Thinking back now on those early years, the difficult things I had to overcome loom large in my memory. They will always be there, a part of me. But that's not the whole story. I also remember with fondness my own awakenings: the teenage romances, the thrill of the ocean and nature, and, maybe most of all, the pangs of curiosity, the love of learning that would lead me, ultimately, to a life in science.

CHAPTER ONE

RAISED IN THREE PARALLEL UNIVERSES

My parents arrived in South Africa in 1936 as newlywed refugees who had escaped the worst of the Nazi atrocities. But their being Jewish in Germany had denied them both a high school education and the career and earning benefits that came with it. My mom and dad came from humble backgrounds back in the Old Country, and their entry into South Africa was made possible only by $100 borrowed from a rich Swiss uncle. One hundred dollars in assets, a small fortune in those days, was the required threshold to be permitted entry into South Africa. But the borrowed funds weren't my parents to keep. Instead, the money was immediately recycled to other relatives in Germany to enable *their* passage to South Africa. This guaranteed my parents' pockets were essentially empty when they arrived. There they were in Cape Town, unable to speak English and relatively uneducated. What must life have been like for them?

They were happy newlyweds, and thankfully, my mom had learned to sew at a "haushaltungsschule," where, during Hitler's ascension, Jewish girls were allowed to study home economics. (Jewish children in Germany were barred from attending regular school.) Fortunately, her talent as a seamstress earned them their keep as they started out in Cape Town. And while it was hard at first to not speak the language (English *or* Afrikaans), it helped that there were other German Jewish immigrants there, a small population they could fall in with. They became part of an isolated ethnic community, separate from the larger community of South African Jews who had come as part of an earlier wave from Lithuania and Russia at the turn of the century. Starting a new life thousands of miles away from their families and all they'd ever known couldn't have been easy. But, of course, they were grateful to have escaped the slaughter that befell so many of their relatives and countrymen back in Germany.

MOM AND DAD AS HAPPY REFUGEES FROM GERMANY, 1938: Ernst and Grete Stern on the beach in Cape Town with their nephew, my first cousin, Gerd Stern, son of Tante (aunt) Alice and Onkel (uncle) Walter.

In South Africa, my mom, Grete, started out by sewing buttonholes for pennies. I mean this literally: She earned a penny per buttonhole. She and my dad, Ernst, lived on that money, part of which he used to buy a pair of socks from a wholesaler and then sell it for a profit. Later, he purchased several pairs of socks, and so began my parents' careers in the "rag trade," as it was then called, which grew to eventually encompass two men's clothing stores, including one on the main street of town, Adderley Street. Like elsewhere in the world, specifically the US, Britain, and the Commonwealth, the clothing, or "schmatta," business provided a niche for Jewish refugees of several generations that required little education or barrier to entry. Although not without its own stigma, the rag trade evolved into the garment industry, which afforded the Jewish refugees who fled persecution a living that allowed them to educate their children and enter the middle class.[2]

The two men's clothing stores were our livelihood throughout my childhood and adolescence. My mom's days were spent at work, but I got to see her in the evenings and on weekends. I cherished these times together; she was warm and attentive and felt like she was all mine. We snuggled often, and I used her satin nightdress as my "lovie" to comfort and help me sleep at night. I called it "mama-nightie" and even still have a few bits of this same well-washed mama-nightie in my possession, one of my most treasured keepsakes. But I have other beautiful memories too, like how she would feed me when I was little and peel grapes for me as I grew older because I disliked the skin. Or how she sewed all my clothes. Or how she'd comfort me when I was upset, often telling me in German that each loss is an opportunity: "Jeder Verlust ist eine Chance." Most of all, I remember how she always made it easy for me to feel strong and smart, fueling that part of me that knows no bounds. I am reminded of the words of a favorite Pulitzer Prize–winning science journalist of mine, Natalie Angier, when describing her childhood: "What worked for me was the expectation

---

2 Adam D. Mendelsohn, *The Rag Race: How Jews Sewed Their Way to Success in America and the British Empire* (New York University Press, 2015).

that I would be smart and responsible. That no matter what you do, you're intelligent. And that was an enormously powerful message."[3]

I just loved being with my mom, but the only ways I got to spend time with her on weekdays was if I went to her store, which was two bus rides away, or she stayed with me on those rare occasions I was home sick. I so loved having her with me on those sick days that as a grown-up, whenever I'm feeling under the weather, strange as it may sound, there's a small but unmistakable joy behind all the hacking and sneezing. And I know that comes from those childhood memories of sick days with my mom. Whenever I see a mom and daughter engaged in an intimate moment, be it at a coffee shop or a concert, I feel warmth tinged with envy.

As for my dad, he was a little trickier. Of course, I knew him for only my first twelve and a half years. But I remember he had a glow about him and sparkling eyes, though he was often silent and distant. The only time he would pay real attention to me was when he took me to soccer (called "football" in South Africa) games. He had been a star soccer player himself as a boy in Germany and later became an official at the Green Point Soccer Club in Cape Town. He would take me to games as a child and carry me like a prize on his shoulders on the sidelines of the field. It made me so happy. And with time, I developed a huge crush on the football players, with their powerful bums and strong legs.

But moments like those with my dad were few and far between. My mom was really my anchor and role model. She was my rock, my ideal of charisma and industriousness. She laughed a lot and had a great sense of humor. To this day, Georges talks of how special she made him feel. She called him "Georgie." I know it was my good fortune to have her as a mom: She was the one who built up the solid half of me, the half that can take on the world and that sits beside my other half, the fragmented half that was tenderized by the immigrant "otherness"—and broken by my father, whose illness and

---

[3] Natalie Angier, *MS Magazine*, Feb/March 2000, 53.

departure by suicide wrenched at my spirit and robbed me of my sense of self-worth.

What *was* my sense of self to begin with? Well, I know my immigrant self-image (combined perhaps with an inherited German work ethic) propelled me to work hard at school. I was indeed a fine student, and my academic success helped elevate me from what I perceived as my second-class status, making me feel less alienated from my peers.

FAMILY PHOTO, 1953: Seventeen years after my parents arrived in South Africa as newlyweds, they celebrated the Bar Mitzvah of their first born, my brother Max. **From L to R:** my dad Ernst, mom Grete, Max, grandma "Oma," and me, age 8.

While I was at school and both my parents at work, my grandmother, Oma, ran the household. Oma took on the role of "hausfrau," German for "housewife." She cooked German food, baked German cakes, and welcomed my brother Max and me home from school each day. We loved Oma dearly. She was our advocate and always protected us when we got in trouble with our mom, like when I smoked a cigarette or Max didn't do his homework. I just wished Oma would cook steak instead of "bratwurst" and bake plain sponge cakes instead of her German "streuselkuchen" and "lindsertorte." They were so different from the South African fare I ate in my friends' homes, and that embarrassed me. In my mind, these German delicacies carried the immigrant label, and my lunch box was my scarlet letter.

Max likely shared some of these feelings, but we are also very different. He is five years older than me, born in 1940. It may sound unkind to point out, but he was a pretty lazy student and, right or wrong, therefore less praised and appreciated in many ways by our parents, although Oma made him feel special. Understandably, my parents' disapproval led Max to resent me, Mommy's "good girl." This made him act less supportive of his little sister than I would have liked. Besides being smart, I was a *girl*, and Max let me feel, from a very young age, all the indignities of being female. For example, he played street soccer in the neighborhood, and I desperately wanted to join in. But girls weren't allowed to play soccer in those days. Max's solution was to make me the goalpost, rooting me to one spot, stiff as a board, and forbidding me from moving or talking. I'm not a good nonparticipant, and so my role left me frustrated.

Our house was in Oranjezicht, a bedroom community in the city of Cape Town with a lovely view of downtown and the bay on one side and stunning Table Mountain on the other. When my parents came home, exhausted from long days at work, we'd eat Oma's dinner together, served by the Black maid, Bessie. After dinner, we would relax by listening to the radio or reading the newspaper. I would play "house" and always pretended to be Mom, with high-heeled shoes and lots of babies. I became obsessed with Queen Elizabeth II's coronation in 1953, treasuring a chintzy facsimile of her horse-drawn carriage with her and the Duke of Edinburgh sitting inside. I'm still fascinated by the British royals to this day. Back then, there was no television available in South Africa because TV was banned under the Apartheid regime, so I got my fix of the royal family from newspapers and magazines.

After dinner each night, my mom would bustle about in her warm and demonstrative way. My dad was quieter and remained in his own bubble. He would sit at a table and count the day's earnings from the stores, reconciling the books. The clothing store he managed, The Man's Shop, was quite elegant and served mainly white people on Adderley Street, Cape Town's main street; it was his pride and joy. My mom managed a branch store, Star Outfitters, in the suburb of Salt River that served mainly non-whites, mixed-race Coloreds, some Black Africans, and the occasional white person. Businesses weren't completely segregated. Quite telling isn't it that while the government flat-out prohibited the crossing of racial lines in almost every other aspect of life, it had less of a problem with money being exchanged and especially with it being passed from brown hands to white ones?

I was fascinated by some of the names of my mom's African customers, like Sunshine and September, and how she would welcome them to the store with a beaming, "Hello, Sunshine! How are the children?" or "Good morning, September, are you over your cold?" Sunshine and September always met my mom with smiles on their faces.

I often wondered about the apparent joyfulness of these Black Africans, whose warmhearted, boisterous personalities left such an impression on me. Not only were they subjected to all the indignities of Apartheid, most were also very poor. Why was it that the wealthier, more privileged whites seemed much less jubilant, sometimes bordering on morose? Cultural differences likely accounted for some of this. Growing up in "kraals," traditional African villages of huts, in their homelands or shantytowns flanking the cities could have certainly provided a more secure feeling than being raised in isolation in suburban houses. Also, many African babies are carried on their mothers' backs until the next sibling is born. What could possibly be better for a baby's emotional development than being on Mom's body from birth through the most formative months of infancy? That's enough to put a smile on anyone's face. As a scientist, of course, I know this to be true. But I also understand that none of these observations about the Black South Africans I knew and loved as a child can or should obfuscate the brutal reality of their lives under a system of entrenched inequality, forced removals from their homes into segregated "Bantustans," and state violence (which progressed into a truly ghastly campaign of militarized terror in the '70s and '80s, after I'd left). Perhaps the very thing that drew me to this third universe—the distinct combination of great personal warmth, dignity, and unbreakable spirit in the face of enormous adversity—was simply a necessary survival mechanism for my conscience in response to enormous human cruelty and deprivation?

To this day, I wrestle with these questions. I know that South Africa's "greatest son," Nelson Mandela, who is very much a hero of mine, famously made a point of finding joy, love, and even laughter during his twenty-seven years of imprisonment, most of which were served at Robben Island in a tiny cell with no bed or proper toilet. Madiba, as he is affectionately referred to by South Africans, was undeniably an extraordinary human being—possessed with a rare, almost unimaginable courage and commitment—who rightfully became a global icon in the vein of Mahatma Gandhi and Dr. Martin Luther King, Jr., almost universally respected for his leadership and contributions to the fight for justice and equality. But perhaps his spirit and humanity are just epic versions of the same spirit and humanity I perceived in my mom's African customers, Bessie, and others?

I did notice a real contrast, temperamentally speaking, between Black South Africans and the second universe I inhabited. My white classmates and their families were more well heeled than my own family, and they were all native English speakers. They were at the top of the social hierarchy where I lived but often seemed oddly subdued, solemn in their mood and bearing. Over the years and decades since leaving South Africa, I've thought about this a lot and tried to unpack the dynamics, mores, and behaviors of my three childhood universes. In particular, I've pondered whether there might be something—guilt, fear, anxiety—behind the more formal, stoic demeanor of the prosperous parents of my white classmates. Or is it just human nature that the more successful a person becomes, the lonelier and less friendly they also become? I don't know the answers. And I certainly didn't have the language or perspective at the time to make sense of it all.

But even as a child, I saw that my mom was different than my friends' moms, livelier, a lot more fun. Unlike them, she had to go to work. And yes, she worked hard in her store and was good at what she did, but she was less consumed by the business than my dad. As soon as she arrived home, she embraced us and engaged with me and Max in her usual warm and animated style. Home was a happy place for me, mainly because of her, Oma, and Bessie, all of whom I loved dearly. In the afternoons, Bessie and I would often spend time together alone in her modest room, which had a separate entrance from the rest of the house. I felt myself surrounded by strong women. Little did I know this strength would soon be tested when our family and household were rocked by an unexpected and unspeakable tragedy.

CHAPTER TWO

A CRASH COURSE IN TRAGEDY AND RESILIENCE

One November evening in 1957, we decided to go on a drive for ice cream, my mom and dad, Oma, Max, and me. November in the southern hemisphere is springtime, so the days were getting warmer and longer. I sat in the back seat of our American Packard with Max and Oma, and my dad periodically reached back from the driver's seat to hold my hand. This was unusually affectionate for him, a welcome change. I wondered what had inspired it, but the thought quickly vanished from my twelve-year-old brain. The next day, however, many more questions arose when we got a call from his shop saying he hadn't shown up to work. "Was he still home?" they asked. No, we told them, he had left as usual that morning.

We proceeded to call around, contacting friends and asking if they knew where he was. Finally, we phoned the police. All we knew at that point was he'd last been seen that morning when he'd given one of his African staff a ride to work. Afterward, he seemed to have disappeared. What could have happened to him? We had no idea, and in the stressful days that followed, we didn't get any closer to finding out.

From there, days became weeks, and weeks became months. Months of sheer agony, filled with vigils, searches, and ever-growing despair as lead after lead turned up empty. Every time the phone rang, my mom startled in anticipation of news. None came. Eventually, she hired a private detective, who combed many thousands of miles by car to try to find my father. My mother even went to séances to have the spirits guide the search. But still, nothing changed. No trace of my dad.

Although Mom's trademark laughter had by then given way to anguish and she was far from her usual vibrant self, our home remained abuzz with family and her friends, who held lots of theories about my father's disappearance. I was grateful for their comforting presence and rarely found myself alone at home. But at school, which was an all-girls school, the Good Hope Seminary High School, there were only silent stares; no one spoke of my father's disappearance, but my teachers and friends surely wondered: *Had Mr. Stern been captured? Had Marlene's father been killed? Was he suffering from amnesia and driving across South Africa?* Amnesia was my favorite theory because it gave me hope he would come home as soon as he regained his memory. But even this fantasy was not enough to buoy me. My self-esteem plummeted to a new low. As if it weren't bad enough to be a child of immigrants, with all that such an identity implied, now I was a child of gossip and scandal, destined to be looked upon with even more shame and pity. At least, that's how my young mind viewed the situation. The local newspapers, *The Cape Times* (the morning paper) and *Cape Argus* (in the afternoons), ran frequent headlines on my dad's disappearance. "Businessman, Father of Two, Vanishes on Way to Work," "Adderley Street Shop Owner Missing for Two Days…a Week…a Month…," and on and on. The humiliation compounded by worry hurt throughout my entire being.

But, no, I told myself, this was only temporary and would all recede after my father returned, which I knew he would. He had to. After all, nothing *really* bad had ever happened to me in my twelve years. I recalled him holding my hand the night before he disappeared; how could he ever leave me?

I held onto hope, clutched it tightly, afraid of what it would mean to let go. During a school holiday about eight months after my father disappeared, my mom arranged for me to go on a little vacation to a farm community, Ceres, in the countryside accompanied by Oma and my favorite aunt, Tante Alice. The thinking was that it might be good for me to just get away for a bit. My mom needed to stay back to mind the stores and wait for my dad's return, which she too believed would happen. She was clinging to hope the same way I was, and she was right that it was good for me to get away from the interminable waiting and searching, not to mention the silent stares of my schoolmates.

Ceres was a fun place to be at the start of the Cape winter because it snowed there, a little in the valleys and much more on the white-capped mountain peaks that famously surround the area. Snow is a rarity in South Africa, so I enjoyed waking up in the morning and going outside to throw snowballs before it all melted in the warmth of the day. We stayed at a country inn that bordered a farm. Each morning, we were awakened early by crowing roosters, and I ran out to help the farmhands feed the chickens and livestock in the new-day snow. After a breakfast of warm, fresh-baked, whole-grain bread with farm butter, eggs, and stewed fruit from the orchards, Tante Alice and I went for long walks among the fruit trees. She was good at girl talk, and we chatted away as we walked among tidy rows of apple and pear trees laden with late-harvest fruit. (As an aside, Ceres fruit juices are now sold worldwide.) I was a million miles away from the tragedy gripping my family as I munched on freshly picked Granny Smith and Golden Delicious apples. We poked around hothouses, where summer fruits grew even in the winter: peaches, plums, apricots, and cherries. I particularly liked the cherries, which I tried to pick in intact pairs and dangle from my ears like earrings. Oma stayed back at the inn, sitting and embroidering with her legs raised because her ankles were swollen from early-stage heart disease.

Afternoons were spent reading and playing board games like checkers, Monopoly (the London version), and Scrabble. After dinner, we sat around a fireplace (no central heating) and played card games:

rummy and "klaberjass" (pronounced club-i-yus), a game with central European roots popular among South African Jews. Then, it was early to bed in preparation for another day and another cycle of refreshing, fun-filled distractions.

I enjoyed the time away with my Oma and my aunt, and after a week, a family friend, Onkel Lothar, came out to Ceres to drive us back home. On the way, we were stuck behind a row of cars at a "robot," what they call traffic lights in South Africa. Street vendors were coming up to the vehicles to sell their wares of Ceres fruits and flowers and Cape Town newspapers, and Onkel Lothar rolled down his window to buy an evening paper from one fellow. But then the light changed, the cars started moving, and Onkel Lothar immediately reached around to the back seat to pass the paper back to us, oblivious of its contents. Always curious, I took the paper and unfolded it. There, on the front page, above the fold, was a picture of a car being pulled out of the Cape Town docks. The car had a man's legs sticking out a window. The legs were those of my father.

We made it through the traffic light and to a red public phone booth. We called home. I don't recall who answered, but it was confirmed that my dad had been found in his car in the Cape Town docks. He had likely driven himself there the morning of his disappearance and been submerged in salt water for eight months. Pickled. All I could imagine was him gasping for air and drowning. The thought was too much to bear. I was devastated. Again, nothing truly bad had ever happened to me, and for months I had been telling myself he'd just suffered amnesia but would regain his memory and come back home. That he'd hold my hand again.

And then, this. It all seemed out of a movie. The way he died and was eventually discovered. The way we found out: on our way home from lovely Ceres, where my spirits *had* been lifted more than I expected by the change in scenery. The whole film reel of this extraordinary episode in my life—our trip to the country, being picked up by Onkel Lothar to go home, and the terrible turn the story then took—became a kind of permanent loop in my brain. To this day, whenever I travel home from a vacation, I feel a strange fear, a sense that something bad awaits. Even apart from vacations, there are times I *should* be happy, when I'm feeling generally excited or optimistic, and yet that good mood is tinged with something I can't quite explain but feels like foreboding. I became aware too early that, in the words of Robert Frost, "Nothing Gold Can Stay."

After leaving the red phone booth, we still had quite a way to drive. Eventually, we arrived home to a throng of people in the house, including my mother and brother Max, who were completely distraught. When Mom finally calmed down, she told us some shocking news: My dad had tried to kill himself once before, with an overdose of sleeping pills. Before that attempt could succeed, he was found and rushed to a hospital, where his stomach was pumped. After an overnight stay, my mother brought him home and acted as if nothing was amiss, implying they'd just been away on a short vacation while Max and I were home with Oma and Bessie. The truth had been completely hidden from us kids. I remembered that "trip" and recalled being pleased that Mom and Dad, who worked *so* hard, had gotten some time away together.

And it wasn't just my dad's previous suicide attempt that had been concealed from us; we had also been kept in the dark about his business woes. Apparently, The Man's Shop was being threatened with loss of lease. This would have been especially tough for my dad given how much of his identity was tied to his fancy store. Why were we not told? Ridiculous as it may seem, I genuinely felt I could have prevented his fate had I only known. Why did he leave us? Was I not worth hanging around for? I was crushed, heartbroken, and ashamed. That is the other half of me.

The funeral, held in the Jewish tradition, was a heart-wrenching affair, as one would expect. We were laying to rest a forty-six-year-old suicide victim. But something else was put to rest that day alongside my father, something no one else could see: my innocence. Now I knew really bad things *can* happen; our worst nightmares *can* come true.

My mother was beside herself with grief during the funeral, so much so that Max and I had to hold her on each side to prop her up. We were all an emotional mess. I was so distraught I have no recollection of the eulogy. What I do remember from the rest of that dreadful day is the rabbi making small rips, or tears, in the mourners' clothes, my mom's, Max's, and mine. I knew the tears in the garments were meant to symbolize the tears in our hearts from losing a loved one. The tear in my heart felt more like a gaping hole. Nonetheless, the rabbi performed the ritual on our garments; mine, a navy-blue sweater that was part of my school uniform.

I remember the coffin being lowered into the grave with hundreds of people surrounding the grave site. I knew my dad was in there, but it also seemed impossible that this person, this body, being put in the ground was the human being I had known my whole life. It *was* him, of course, but I had a hard time believing what I was seeing. I tried to snap myself back to reality. Once the coffin was in place at the bottom of the grave, some of the men (only men, per tradition) were called upon to shovel soil, three heaps each, into the grave. Thud. Thud. Thud. I was numb and sobbing. The sounds of the soil hitting the coffin reverberate to this day.

Finally, we were driven home, where we observed shiva, the traditional Jewish seven days of mourning. All the mirrors in the house were covered, we recited daily prayers, and my mom, brother, and I sat all day on low stools, receiving well-wishers who brought food and were our constant companions. But then, abruptly, it seemed, the seven days were over, and it was back to the normal routine. I knew the shiva had to end but wanted to keep remembering and honoring my father. I sewed the tear in my sweater, which, as I said, was part of my school uniform, and wore it to school every day for a month as I faced the world. But *facing the world* had a different timbre to it now. Somehow, it felt more natural to be the bereaved daughter of a father who had died than the child of a man who had disappeared and was nowhere to be found. The shame had lessened; my father was dead. And while you never fully recover from the suicide of a loved one, I could face my friends again. Death was better than uncertainty.

CHAPTER THREE

A WIDER WORLD—AND A NEW FAMILY MEMBER

GOOD HOPE, 1961: In high school, I studied hard but also had lots of fun, which is just what I needed after the terrible loss of my father. Gym class was always a blast.

I resumed life as a regular teenager, still studying hard but mingling more now with both girls and boys. My mom remained shaken but took pleasure in both my academic achievements at Good Hope High and my social life, my steady stream of teenage friends. The girls were my classmates at Good Hope High, and the cool guys came from Sea Point Boys High in a different part of town. Some of those girls and boys remain my friends to this day, more than sixty years on. Outside of studying, my time was spent reading, drawing, playing sports, and styling the hair of my girlfriends who donned bouffant hairdos, popularized in the early 1960s by America's glamorous new first lady, Jacqueline Kennedy. I would also go to the beautiful beaches of the Atlantic or Indian Oceans at the tip of Africa, eating frozen "granadilla lollies," as passion fruit popsicles were known, and slathering myself in olive oil to get the deepest tan possible. No sunscreen; no knowledge of the mortal danger of skin cancer. I also watched professional soccer and dated the Sea Point boys. Partying was big, as was cheap wine drunk from gallon-sized, glass liquor bottles with finger holes. If you were really cool, you drank the wine with the bottle perched on your shoulder and held tenuously at the finger hole.

At seventeen, I graduated from high school and entered the Bachelor of Science program at the University of Cape Town (UCT). The application process was simple: Either your grades were good enough to go to the local university, UCT, or they weren't, in which case you could apply to a technical college or school of accounting. But before university began, I went on a trip abroad with my mom, Oma, and Tante Alice: four women traveling together, feeling happy and strong. We visited Oma's brothers and their families in New York City and stayed with them on 142nd Street and Broadway in Harlem, Upper Manhattan, for about a month. I was captivated by the diversity of culture surrounding us in New York and amazed by, of all things, the fact that Americans didn't darn their socks but rather threw them away. In New York, I felt a bit lonesome but also happy, riding the subway alone and gallivanting downtown to explore shops, museums, and the theater. What an eye-opener. New York, New York!

RABBI EUGENE AND MRS. GRETE DUSCHINSKY, 1962: Five years after losing my father, my mother found a new mate. Though it took a little while for me to get used to the idea of her remarrying, to an orthodox rabbi no less, they made each other happy.

While in Manhattan, my mom tried reaching Rabbi Duschinsky, a former rabbi of our congregation in South Africa who had left Cape Town for the US before my father disappeared. She wanted to share her tragedy with the rabbi but was told he was in Israel. Coincidentally, Israel was to be our next stop after leaving New York and passing through London and Paris. Once in Israel, we spent some time sightseeing in Jerusalem, Tel Aviv, and Haifa and visiting distant relatives. I recall quite a bit of laughter among Mom, Oma, Tante Alice, and me on this leg of our trip and was happy my mom was beginning to feel less grief-stricken by the loss of my dad. After all, it had been five years. Then, on a trip between Haifa and Tel Aviv, in a communal taxi called a "sheroot," we were jabbering, and the driver stopped to drop off a passenger and pick up another. The boarding passenger was striking, with a gray beard, black suit, and hat—he was clearly an orthodox Jew. Mom nudged me and said, "That's Duschinsky."

"C'mon, Mom, you're hallucinating," I replied. It turned out she was right; it was him.

The remaining days in Israel were unusual in that Oma, Tante Alice, and I busied ourselves independently of my mom. My bright, beautiful mother went on excursions with the learned, chubby Duschinsky, called "the Rabbi" by all. Much to my dismay, Mom and the Rabbi were falling in love. Although he was smart and open-minded, the idea of a religious presence in our lives was distasteful to me, a committed atheist who believed in evolution and the power of science and not in any god. But their affair continued. This was against the objections of many family and Mom's friends who had heard that the Rabbi had two failed marriages in his past and a nasty reputation as a philanderer with questionable family values and ethics. Despite opposition from family and friends, my mom and the Rabbi were married several months later, and he moved into our house in Oranjezicht.

It was a big change. But a lot seemed to have changed over the past several months. Something had shifted in me during our travels. I felt uplifted, less inferior. I was beginning to shake the child-of-immigrants mentality. I had been excited to meet new people, experience different cultures, explore New York, and get a feel for Israel, a country that loomed large in the imagination of Jewish refugees like my family ("next year in Jerusalem" was a common expression). My experiences abroad had given me a sense of panache; I began to fancy myself "the cosmopolitan girl." And in a way, I was. After all, I had been to the top of the Empire State Building, seen the changing of the guard at Buckingham Palace, been inside the Moulin Rouge, and floated on the Dead Sea. None of my peers had yet ventured abroad. The trip felt like the great equalizer, a catalyst in my ongoing attempt to *overcome*. It had lightened the proverbial chip on my shoulder: the immigrant hang-up, the shame of the rag trade, the humiliation of Oma's poor English and my mom's heavy accent, the embarrassment of German pastries, and the infamy of my father's disappearance and suicide. My travels gave me confidence and, in my mind, put me on par with the children of doctors, lawyers, and even the mayor of Cape Town.

I still thought about my father, but it wasn't with the same acute pain as before. And I was happy to see his store, The Man's Shop, live to see another day, moving from its original rental property to a small building my mom had purchased (each loss is an opportunity). Soon, I would be off to university, and my brother Max, now twenty-two, would take care of the shop.

Max was quite the playboy in those days. He dated many different young women and was particularly captivated by nurses. He was also doing a masterful job at The Man's Shop. He could look at a customer as they walked into the store and know their exact suit size down to the length of the pants, the mark of an outstanding salesman. He bought a white Studebaker with tail fins, a fancy American car, and gave me his old, red Alfa Romeo. I used the car to drive to UCT daily, feeling like quite the glamour girl in a red Alfa.

As for my mom, she was happy in her new life with the Rabbi, at least for the first few years. He was in love with a beautiful, capable woman and she with his intellectual depth and high standing in the Jewish community. He was the "Av Beth Din," the head of the Rabbinical Court of the Union of Orthodox Hebrew Congregations in Cape Town. Living together, the four of us plus Oma and Bessie, wasn't always easy; we had our share of growing pains. But we made the best of it, and part of me was relieved my mom had found a new partner.

By this point, I had warmed to the Rabbi myself. I appreciated how he engaged with me as a young scholar, and I admired his philosophical bent. We enjoyed a mutual respect. He was born in Hungary, the latest in a long tradition of rabbinical elites educated in Prague, London, and New York. He was undeniably a peculiar man: rotund, with a big belly, strange eating habits, and a formality that felt odd to us. Also, some questionable ethics of his surfaced much later, after Mom's death, having to do with money Max and I loaned him from my mom's estate. Nevertheless, while she was alive, we made do and coexisted peacefully with the Rabbi. Thankfully, he didn't try to push his faith onto me. I was free to live a secular life. But I actually ended up enjoying our talks about religion and philosophy. About evolution and science too, which had always been my passions and were soon to become my calling.

CHAPTER FOUR

FALLING IN LOVE *AND* FALLING IN LOVE WITH SCIENCE

My last year of high school was thrilling, with me falling in and out of love with various Sea Point boys. There was much dancing, dating, hand-holding, partying, and smooching, as well as some drinking and smoking, both tobacco and "dacha" (Afrikaans for "marijuana"). This was the early 1960s, a pretty wild time for youth globally. We danced exuberantly to the rock 'n' roll music of Elvis Presley and The Beach Boys (and slowed down to the admittedly less hip songs of Doris Day). We were also starting to listen to the American folk music of Joan Baez, Bob Dylan, and Buffy Sainte-Marie. I was still a serious student and had become very keen on biology, fascinated by evolution and the inner workings of living organisms, from microbes to men.

The seeds of this passion were planted in me early on. I recall lying in the bathtub at maybe five or six years old and marveling at the sheer fact that I was alive, noticing all the bodily functions I usually took for granted. It struck me, maybe for the first time, that I was a living creature who could breathe, move, and feel (which I confirmed by pinching my skin), categorically different from my toy dolls, who couldn't do any of those things. That intrigued me. I also puzzled over what those dolls were made of, so I took a few and dissected them, cutting into their bellies and dismembering them, much to my mother's horror. It took her a while to realize that curiosity, rather than sadism, was driving me.

The breathtaking physical beauty of Cape Town captivated me too: the mountains; the oceans; the blinding sunlight; the puffy, white clouds against a bright, blue sky; and the restless breeze that sometimes intensified to a gale-force wind. Then, there was the extraordinary array of wildlife on land and in the sea, from gazelles frolicking on the mountain slopes to the occasional ostrich prancing on a dirt road in the countryside. Growing up where I did, surrounded by oceans, I was equally enraptured by marine life. I watched fish while bathing in the warm Indian Ocean and was curious how they knew to swim in schools, and while swimming on a rocky, cold Atlantic Ocean beach, I wondered what made the sea anemone clasp my finger when I poked it. I found so much awe-inspiring beauty in these remarkable organisms but was also left with more questions than answers.

The area's vegetation cast a similar spell over me. I loved to gaze up at the tall, wild oaks and the stunning contrast they drew to all the groomed vineyards, with their rows of grapevines. I wondered about their beautiful colors and waxy leaves. Why? How? A favorite spot of mine to visit was a botanical garden on the slopes of Table Mountain called Kirstenbosch. I loved to walk and explore the sprawling natural beauty of the garden with my mom, holding hands all the while. Sometimes, I also got to go to Kirstenbosch on school tours with teachers and school friends. The gardens are both wild and cultivated, featuring plants indigenous to South Africa, including brilliant and majestic aloe, Strelitzia (birds of paradise), and proteas. I was especially drawn to the hydrangeas—bright pink, mauve, and blue. They bloom in the height of summer, which in South Africa is December, and are therefore called "Christmas Flowers." I spent hours drawing the different cells I found inside leaves I dissected and placed under a microscope. I wanted to see further, right into those cells. This was the very first impulse I had to become a molecular biologist. Much as artists like Georgia O'Keeffe and Yayoi Kusama take their inspiration from nature, scientists can too.

While molecular biology was where my scientific curiosity was leading me, I needed to be proficient in chemistry and physics to study biology. However, Good Hope High was an all-girls school, and unfortunately, receiving an adequate education in chemistry and physics was not an option at an all-girls school in the 1950s. Those subjects weren't even offered, and although we studied algebra, geometry, and trigonometry, we did not learn calculus. There were three paths offered to us: the academically disengaged girls could study domestic science (home economics), those interested in becoming secretaries could study bookkeeping and typing, and the academically inclined could study language. I was in that third bucket—language—and my choices were French or Latin. I selected Latin, which I took along with the core courses of history, biology, the abovementioned math, English, and Afrikaans, in which we needed to be fluent to graduate high school and enter university. The dearth of options certainly left me and other female students at an academic disadvantage, but sadly, that was the norm back then.

It wasn't all bleak, though. Going to an all-girls school was also very empowering for me in its own way. The leaders were all women as were the laggards. There was no gender-based performance bias. The all-female environment also imbued me with a sense of strength and command that prepared me to navigate a male-dominated world. For example, I was appointed prefect, which was a position given to final-year high school students that granted them special responsibilities and authorized them to enforce the school rules. A bit like a hall monitor but with more authority and prestige. And though the power was not my end goal, I relished the experience of not just an all-female environment but the taste of leadership in a context where gender wasn't a factor.

PREFECTS AT GOOD HOPE HIGH, 1962: Going to an all-girls high school was empowering, even though it meant I couldn't take chemistry or physics. I thrived at Good Hope and in my final year was selected, along with these classmates, to be a prefect (that's me four rows up on the left).

For better or worse, being in a community of women also immunized me against sensing discrimination when I was treated poorly as an adult because in my youth, there had been no gender attribution to bad conduct. That blind spot put me in a uniquely strong position as I crisscrossed a world dominated by men who, all too often, were prone to gender bias. I fought back when injustices were heaped upon me but was mostly oblivious to prejudices related to my being a woman. Ironic as it may seem, this obliviousness kept me from becoming rattled and obsessed with gender discrimination and instead allowed me to feel sturdy, focusing on the task at hand and getting on with the job.

Just before graduating high school, I was studying trigonometry for my matric when a fateful encounter changed the course of my life. "Matric" referred to a set of exams administered in one's last year of high school by the South African government. You had to pass with high grades if you wanted to be accepted to the local university (UCT), which was, again, pretty much the only game in town. I knew how important these tests were and studied day and night in preparation (they call this type of intense studying "swotting" in South Africa). I was in this deep study mode, sitting at the dining-room table in my pajamas with my trig textbook and notes spread across the tabletop, when my brother walked in with two pals: a friend from Jo'burg (Johannesburg) and a friend of the Jo'burg friend. I immediately recognized the friend of the friend as Georges Belfort, a guy I had known and had a big crush on since I was thirteen.

We first met on Clifton beach, and I was immediately struck by how handsome and smart he was. Georges had asked me how old I was. He was eighteen at the time, and I confessed to being "only thirteen." He then placed his hand on the pocket of his swim trunks and made a gesture as if pulling out a coin. "Here's a ticky," he said. "Give me a call when you graduate high school." A "ticky" was the equivalent of a dime, and those were the days of phone booths, when tickies were the currency of flirtation. Now, almost five years later, I couldn't believe the same handsome charmer had suddenly appeared in my dining room. "Play it cool, Marlene," I told myself.

"Oh, it's unusual to see a girl swotting trig," Georges said. I tried to hide my embarrassment at my appearance on what was undoubtedly the ugliest day of my life. I was exhausted from swotting, with zits covering my face and rings under my eyes. Ugh. In contrast, he looked gorgeous to me. "You'll need to do many examples from the back of the book," he said. "Solve as many problems as you can, and you'll be fine." He was an advanced chemical engineering student at UCT at the time, so I knew he knew what he was talking about. I timidly thanked him for his advice to try to stop him from asking me any more trig questions. Then, he gave me his phone number, in case I needed help with the trig problems, and I reminded him about the "ticky" conversation from years earlier. He smiled and left.

Shortly after our ugliest-day-of-my-life encounter, Georges called and told me how impressed he was with my grasp of trig and invited me on a date to a concert by Roy Castle, a popular British singer. During the concert, he reached for my hand, sending chills down my spine and goose bumps all over my arms. That was the start of a serious, passionate, and committed relationship. Georges would visit often, taking two buses from Sea Point to Oranjezicht to be with me. Or my mom would drive me to Sea Point to visit "Georgie," with whom she developed a warm and loving relationship. Georges lived in a modest apartment with his single mom. He played rugby and serious chess, and he read *Time* magazine cover to cover every week to find out what was going on in Europe and the US. I was besotted with him.

Meanwhile, I still needed to get up to speed in physics and chemistry to be prepared for my Bachelor of Science studies at UCT. My mom had the idea of hiring Georges as my tutor; after all, he could use the money. It worked out well. He was an excellent teacher; his explanations of complicated material were clear as bells. After our lessons, Georges would use his earnings to take me for an ice cream or to "bioscope" (the movies).

Who could have known this tutoring arrangement would mark the start of us exploring science and life together, Georges and me? Occasionally, he would ask me to proofread something he'd written, and I liked that. I will have a lot more to say in the chapters ahead about what it meant to pursue both science *and* life together. But I bring it up here because this was the seed of a partnership and a way of thinking about the partnership that persists to this day—with my contributions obviously growing stronger over the years than what they were when I was a tender seventeen years old.

Once I entered UCT, I was among the less than 10 percent of students out of the three hundred total studying science or premed who were female, but I soldiered on and performed well. Indignities were many, as when I was busily pipetting in a chemistry lab and an obnoxious teaching assistant (a "demonstrator" in local parlance), whom I'll refer to as Laurence K., confronted me by saying, "Miss Stern, what are you doing here?" I looked at him, baffled. He said, "Didn't you know that women are for maternity, *not* chemistry?" I was stunned but continued pipetting. Dumbstruck! But I got on with it and completed the lab. Fast-forward fifteen years, three children, and a PhD to when I land a job as a research scientist at the New York State Department of Health in Albany in 1978. On my first day, as I walk into my new workplace, I happen by an office with the name Laurence K. on the door. Sure enough, we had arrived at the same place seven thousand miles from UCT, and I was able to tell Laurence that women could be for both maternity *and* chemistry. I was triumphant.

Despite the bias against female science students at UCT, I performed well, and for that one year when Georges and I overlapped, we were together at every opportunity. I loved my science classes, and Georges was a huge help, continuing to tutor me, holding my hand both physically and academically. By then, my understanding of chemistry was strong enough to ace those courses on my own, but I still needed his help with physics. My scholastic success and Georges's adoration boosted my self-esteem and helped me heal, making whole the wounded child battered by foreign beginnings and traumatic loss. Between classes, we met at the student union for lunch or outside, where we'd bask in the sun together. What did we talk about back then? Well, one thing I distinctly remember is how we'd worry whenever my period was late, having given my virginity to him. Close friends of ours had been forced to have a shotgun wedding, and we didn't want that for ourselves.

We talked a lot about our studies, of course. We often danced; Georges is an exceptional dancer, combining a keen sense of rhythm with creative movement. We also discussed the injustices of Apartheid and the disenfranchisement of the majority of the South African population. On campus, there were very few students of color. They were mainly confined to the Black townships and brown suburbs, with their own universities of inferior quality. As I mentioned earlier, our main exposure to Black and "Colored" people was through the service industry, working in our homes and businesses. We felt acutely aware of our relative privilege, but our hands were mostly tied unless we were prepared to go to jail because the lid was kept on student activism by the white Apartheid government. Arrests of students opposed to Apartheid were common. We were afraid and felt impotent to do anything to repair the racial and social injustices we saw.

One day, Georges told me his friend Michael Schneider, who gave him a ride to UCT every day, had disappeared. Not long after, we heard the police had found explosives in Michael's garage and he was suspected of being part of a Jewish resistance group planning to blow up the houses of parliament in Cape Town. There was a manhunt for him, and a long while later, we read in the papers he had fled South Africa and found political asylum in London. Scary stuff.

UCT GRADUATES, EARLY 1960s: Marlene and Georges at the start of our lifelong collaboration. Three years after seeing Georges graduate as a chemical engineer, I received my BS degree and a year later an honors degree (master's equivalent) in physiology/biochemistry and microbiology.

Georges was as deeply opposed to Apartheid as I was, and this combined with the limited future available to scientists in South Africa compelled him to leave for the US after graduating from UCT as a chemical engineer. I was heartbroken, but my psyche was intact, and we agreed to see each other in a few years, after I graduated from

UCT. Meanwhile, we were free to date other people, and I continued to pursue my scientific studies, which I felt confident I could now handle on my own.

CHAPTER FIVE

FINDING ONE'S PLACE IN THE WORLD

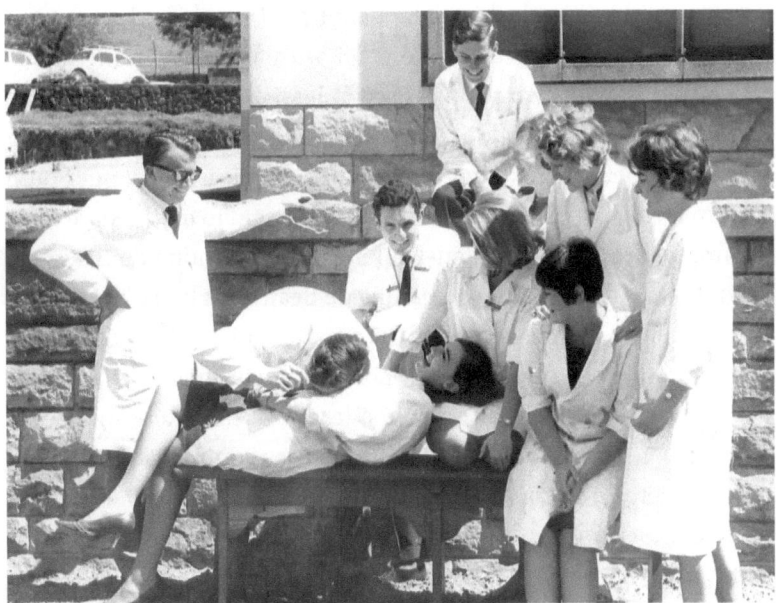

UCT, 1966: Most of my work toward my honors degree was at the UCT Medical School, where it was fun to clown around, lying on the bench, with the physiology/biochemistry students.

Several other relationships (one serious) and three years later, I graduated—first with my BSc (BS) degree and the next year with an honors degree, the equivalent of a US master's, in physiology/biochemistry and microbiology. Those latter years were spent at the medical school, where I enjoyed both the course content and my fellow students. From there, I spent 1967 traveling to Israel, the UK, then Southern California to visit Georges. In Israel, I worked as a lab tech at the internationally renowned Weizmann Institute of Science in Rehovot, where I caught my first glimpses of world-class scientists and other famous people. The Weizmann, named after Russian biochemist and first president of Israel Chaim Weizmann, is a national showcase and on the Israeli celebrity–tourist circuit. I worked in the lab of Professor Michael Sela, a rock star of immunology. I was trembling when I first met him. All the professors I'd ever known had been intimidating in their formal jackets and ties, often bow ties. I stammered, "I'm honored to meet you, Professor Sela," to which he disarmingly replied, "Call me Micha-el," in a strong Polish/Israeli accent and open-neck shirt. The next time I saw him, I was standing in the lab at a spectrophotometer with a cuvette in my hands. He walked in with two people, each at least a head shorter than he and rather unassuming looking, the woman in a turban. Gesturing toward me, he turned to the couple and said, "Please meet our South African technician, Marlene Stern." Then he said to me, "Please meet my friends from France, Jean-Paul Sartre and Simone de Beauvoir." Whoa! I was in the middle of reading de Beauvoir's book *The Second Sex* at the time. I almost dropped the cuvette. This was the big leagues and my first exposure to world-renowned intellectuals.

The Weizmann was also my first lesson in the internationalism of science. Scientists and students from every continent worked and trained there. One could sense the collaborative spirit, but also the fierce competition, among trainees from around the globe. I lived with students and post-docs in a campus dorm called Clore House, where we socialized some. But I was fundamentally lonely, missing my mother and friends and feeling isolated because of how few women there were among the trainees—maybe 3 percent were women. Also, the residents of Clore House were students and post-docs working with an intellectual intensity that made me uncomfortable as a technician. I felt inferior. My childhood insecurities raised their ugly heads again.

But it was really the loneliness that wore at me—a loneliness felt by many of us foreign trainees, not just the women. Each day at about 11:00 a.m., we all left our labs and walked over to Clore House to check for mail from home. This was before the internet, and it took weeks for handwritten letters and postcards sent via air mail to arrive from South Africa or other parts of the world. We were thrilled if we received a letter and sat on the benches around the mail cubbies to read it immediately. I desperately wanted to receive letters from my mother and Georges, having all but forgotten the other guys I had dated. There we would sit, eyes moving left to right over the page—or right to left or top to bottom depending on our national origin. If we received no mail, we trekked back to our respective labs, feeling downhearted.

Thankfully, I had a lot of exciting things to look forward to. My next stop was London on my way to the US to see Georges. There, in South Kensington, I roomed with two South African flatmates: my friends Sandra Wyner and Charlotte Hinder. They both came from wealthy families and had plenty of leisure time, but I needed to work, which I did, first as a chambermaid then as a teacher, so my social life was limited. Sandra and Charlotte were as rabidly anti-Apartheid and socially conscious as I was, so occasionally I joined them at anti-Apartheid rallies. It felt liberating to protest the racial and social injustices of South Africa after having been constrained by the oppressive regime while living there. I would also squeeze in time to visit the local museums—the Victoria and Albert Museum in our neighborhood, the Tate and the Jewel House at the Tower of London.

My job as a chambermaid at a local B&B was a defining experience in and of itself. It seemed a good way to bide my time while I waited for a work permit that would allow me to teach high school science.

My days started at 5:00 a.m. with waiting breakfast tables. The B&B guests were tourists and football (soccer) players from out of town. I had a soft spot for soccer and for the players, so I was excited to work where I could interact with the sport and its athletes. But instead of responding to my knowledge of soccer and discussing the games of the day with me, the guys humored me with snide remarks about the size of my breasts or the color of my eyes. Instead of taking my knowledge and diligence seriously, they poked fun at my South African accent.

After clearing the breakfast tables, I worked off some of my hurt and frustration by cleaning the rooms as well as humanly possible. I felt a sense of accomplishment when the bathroom smelled fresh after wiping away urine stains or scraping vomit from the floors. But rather than praising me for sanitizing the filth, the Persian hotel owner was verbally abusive and put me down for not being more efficient with my time. I swallowed tears, composed myself, and took long walks around London in the afternoons. During these walks, I decided I needed to make a future for myself in a field where diligence and intelligence were rewarded and I would be treated with respect. I started to think about a life in science. But I felt conflicted because of the lack of women in the field, never having had a female professor in all my years at UCT. So, I put off making any decisions and continued my travels.

After London, it was on to New York City. Arriving on a humid, midsummer day, I remember the condensation on the soles of the metallic sandals I had purchased in London. My feet slid forward, and I almost slipped as I walked down the gangplank of the plane. Another of my purchases, this one for Georges, was the newly released Beatles album *Sgt. Pepper's Lonely Hearts Club Band*. After passing through customs, relieved the agents hadn't discovered the pot hidden in the tampons in my luggage (what was I thinking?), I made my way back to my Harlem relatives, Onkel Max (Oma's brother) and Tante Regina, on 142nd Street. Having visited them several years earlier with my mom, I knew what to expect of the neighborhood, but that had been in winter, and nothing prepared me for the summer stench of accumulated garbage in the streets or the smell of urine in the stairwell of their building. After hiking up three flights of stairs with heavy luggage, hugging my great-uncle and -aunt, and eating some streuselkuchen Tante Regina had baked for me, I dashed to the phone to call Georges in California. It turned out, he already had *Sgt. Pepper*—I had been hoping to introduce him to the landmark LP everyone was talking about—but I overcame the disappointment with the thought that in just a few days, we'd be together.

On the flight to Los Angeles, I reflected on the list of boyfriends with whom I'd had more-or-less-serious relationships in Cape Town, Johannesburg, Tel Aviv, and London over the four years Georges and I had been apart. I didn't regret any of them, but Georges was still the love of my life. His intellect, scientific acumen, assertive charm, political persuasion, and good looks captivated me. As the plane started its descent into LA, I prettied myself up nervously, my heart thumping, and wondered if I would still feel the same passion. Perhaps more importantly, would he? I also thought about my mom, how lonely she must have been without me and how I missed her more than ever, now from a distance of ten thousand miles.

My plans were to stay with Georges in Costa Mesa, California, for a few months and then return home to Cape Town. It was 1967, and the Vietnam War was escalating. Georges and I were vehemently opposed to the war. Georges, already a US citizen, now worked for McDonnell Douglas developing fuel cells, desalination units, and water purification systems for spacecraft. Because McDonnell Douglas is a US Army contractor, he was exempt from being drafted. At the time, he was also an engineering master's student at the University of California at Irvine (UCI), then a brand-new campus in the UC system. Meanwhile, I was confused and conflicted about many aspects of my life. The political situation in South Africa was worse than ever. But America seemed to be coming apart at the seams because of the Vietnam debacle. I still adored science but was troubled by the paucity of women in the field and knew it would be a difficult career path to follow. Above all, I was longing for and feeling duty bound to my mother but also desperately in love with Georges, who had decided to make his life in the US. However, this last point was strictly academic given that Georges, who was kind and passionate toward me, had given no signs of wanting to get married, despite my obvious desire to wed. So, I put my quandaries on the back burner and prepared to live with uncertainty for a while.

Georges and I traveled around California, talking a lot about careers and his intention to study for a PhD at UCI. I expressed my ambivalence about academic science versus something more female friendly. I loved to paint and draw. Maybe I could be a teacher of science and art? Or a scientific illustrator? But my decision depended somewhat on whether Georges and I had a future together, so I asked him if he'd marry me. He told me he was considering it and would let me know once he had made up his mind. The days passed, and when I reminded him I was awaiting his decision, he assured me he'd not forgotten and would let me know as soon as he had decided.

We went on to visit Disneyland in Anaheim, where there was a General Electric exhibit showing appliances and equipment of the future, including (presciently!) a phone that allowed you to see the person you were talking to. Imagine that! In contrast to our sleek smartphones, it was one of those old-fashioned rotary phones with a coiled cord that featured a screen attached to the base; but basically, the kernel of the idea was there, outlandish as it seemed at the time. Georges and I were holding hands and discussing how far out some of these futuristic visions were, when out of the blue, he asked, "Will you marry me?" I stood startled, rooted to the ground as I looked at him and he at me. The moment is frozen in my memory forever, though I don't recall my exact answer. It was some form of an excited and resounding "Yes!" I suppressed my thoughts of my mom, the idea of breaking the news and the sadness of leaving her, and instead traveled to Northern California with Georges. From there, we made our way to Nevada, where we stayed in Las Vegas with a man named Tom Perno, who had been a friend of Georges's roommate Tony Mucci. Tony, a brilliant mathematician also at McDonnell Douglas, was from an Italian neighborhood in South Philadelphia, and he and Tom were childhood friends. Tom was a blackjack dealer, so we gambled a bit, but as we had only limited funds, we made only small bets. Although Georges had a real job, he was supporting his mother, Sophie, in Cape Town. And we still needed to plan a wedding. I wasn't much for formal weddings, and when I saw all the justices of the peace in Las Vegas, I decided we could get married then and there and avoid all the fuss. Georges wouldn't hear of it, but Tom liked the idea. So, Tom and I cooked up a plan, got Georges to have a few drinks, and took him to a justice of the peace, with Tom as a witness, but as soon as Georges realized what was going on, he bolted. "I just can't do this to Sophie," he said. I was disappointed but resigned. Initial disagreement before arriving at consensus is part of the fabric of our relationship.

LAS VEGAS, 1967: Newly engaged, Georges and I were full of excitement about building a life together—tinged with some sadness over having to tell my mother I would be leaving South Africa for California.

Georges marked our engagement in Las Vegas by buying me a shocking-pink hat with feathers! That was instead of a diamond ring, I imagine. I did eventually receive a gold wedding band from Georges, but never a diamond. Diamonds are too conventional an expression of love for Georges. I understand where he's coming from. I have a similar attitude around a different convention: Mother's Day. For me, every day is Mother's Day, so why do I need a special day? In fact, all the fuss people make over that one single day kind of irritates me. Likewise, I knew I was the love of Georges's life, so did we really need a diamond to mark that fact? I feel the same way about the annual expectation of grand gestures for Valentine's Day. Why? Who made these rules anyway? For me and Georges, chocolates, roses, and other traditional romantic trappings do not feature prominently in our relationship, but I am just fine with that. It's the daily niceties that are important to us. What matters is the connection, which, I'm happy to report, is as strong now as it was back in 1967, when I was head over heels for the man I would soon marry.

But as excited as I was about our upcoming nuptials, the feeling was bittersweet because it would almost certainly mean making a home half a world away from my mom. The day I finally plucked up the courage to write her a letter breaking the news that Georges and I planned to marry was one of the saddest of my life. I sat on the bed with tears falling onto the blue "aerogram" explaining that we would come to Cape Town to marry and she could then join us in California and live near us, which was, of course, an unrealistic possibility. She was tied to Cape Town by her livelihood, those two men's clothing stores, and her close circle, who had supported her through years of immigration, struggle, and grief. For all these reasons, the thought of my leaving her was more wrenching for her sake than for mine. So, you can imagine my relief when she responded with a telegram sent via Western Union expressing her excitement to arrange a wedding for us and instructing us to leave it all to her, which we did. Four hundred guests later, we were married on December 28, 1967, under the brilliant summer sun of Cape Town.

PART TWO

MOTHER AND SCIENTIST

"If I had a public voice, it was as a scholar, and I shied away from putting too much of myself on the line."

—Jill Ker Conway, *A Woman's Education*

As a young girl, I thought I might like to become a scientist. But what I was certain I *needed* to become was a mom. I wasn't quite sure how I'd pull off succeeding at both these roles, given that I hadn't been exposed to a single female scientist, let alone a scientist who was also a mom. So, I did what I'm good at: I muddled through. Shortly after starting graduate school in Southern California, I stopped taking birth-control pills and became pregnant. That was a purely joyful moment, but I shared it only with family, afraid if any of my thesis committee members discovered my secret, I would flunk my qualifying exam, which was an oral exam and therefore somewhat subject to the impulses of my all-male examiners. There were few female graduate students, let alone pregnant ones.

What was striking during my training was that, while I was an anomaly in the US academic system, I was much more a part of the norm as a post-doctoral fellow in Jerusalem, Israel, where the family-first sentiment prevails. That experience grounded me to the point where I gave birth to two more children while there, feeling well supported by the subsidized Israeli childcare system. As a result, I felt perfectly entitled to be a mom *and* a scientist to the extent that when we returned to the US after my training and I took my first position as a scientist, I had the confidence to pull off both roles.

Although my job proved to be a very mixed experience, with exciting discoveries blended with soul-crushing discrimination, I prevailed, raising three healthy sons while earning scientific recognition. When the nest began to empty as the boys went off to college and I reflected on my dual success in science and motherhood, it occurred to me my satisfaction in parenting and involvement in high-level science were intertwined and mutually beneficial. I realized that rather than shying away from putting too much of myself on the line, I needed to get myself out there and encourage young people (women and men alike) inclined toward having children—not everyone is, and that's fine!—to allow their scholarship to rest on a bed of fulfilled parenthood.

CHAPTER SIX

A BABY, AND A CAREER

Georges was accepted into the PhD program in engineering on the fledgling UCI campus for September 1968, and as soon as we returned from Cape Town, we moved into UCI married student housing at Verano Place in Irvine. Although I was ecstatic to be with Georges, I longed for home and felt totally foreign, the child of immigrants and now an immigrant myself. I could speak English, of course, but the nuances of language were quite different, and I felt like I'd arrived on another planet. An outsider, yet again. Georges was still working full time at McDonnell Douglas, a job he needed to avoid being drafted into the Vietnam War, while also taking evening courses in patent law at University of California, Los Angeles Extension, an hour's drive away. He'd leave for work early in the morning and arrive home late at night at least three nights a week after the long drive from LA County. I would wait all day for him to return, feeling disheartened and struggling to assimilate. I didn't know a soul and barely dared to venture out. Even the most elementary tasks seemed beyond me, like purchasing a few items for the kitchen. When I asked for the crockery (tableware) and cutlery (silverware) departments, the salespeople looked at me like I had just flown in from Mars.

At this point, I already wanted to become a mom but chose to hedge my bets and, somewhat ambivalently, decided to apply to the PhD program in molecular biology at UCI. To complete my application, I needed to take the Graduate Record Exam. Given that UCI was so new, the closest testing center was at the University of Southern California in LA. Georges drove me up to LA one Saturday morning, and I was understandably nervous because I had never taken a multiple-choice standardized test before. However, I had worked through a few GRE preparation manuals and was buoyed by the knowledge that I tested well. I walked into the testing center, picked up the blue test booklet, and was shown to a chair, where I waited with a large group of confident-looking American students to be told to start the exam. The rest of the group flipped up the side-flaps on their chairs and placed their booklets down on their desks. A few minutes later, we were told we could start the two-hour exam. But I had never seen one of those side-flaps before, let alone knew how the flip mechanism worked. I fumbled and became progressively flustered. Eventually, the proctor came to the rescue. I was mortified but sheepishly thanked him and calmed myself by reading the passages in the booklet. I was impressed by the quality of the writing, but as I was beginning to answer the first comprehension questions, the proctor announced, "Ten minutes to go!" Oh, no. I was only about halfway through the exam, having leisurely perused the text without a clue that time was of the essence. Then, with many test questions still unanswered, came the dreaded, "Time's up. Put down your pencils."

I walked out of the testing center in a flood of tears and found Georges waiting for me in his car. He had brought me lunch. I sobbed and sputtered that I had fared so poorly in the general exam that I couldn't possibly sit for the quantitative and special subject (biology) exams that afternoon. He hugged me and said, "Len, c'mon. Give yourself a break. You've never taken a standardized test before. There's a strategy to these tests of pacing oneself. By this afternoon, you'll be feeling better, you'll know how to operate the chair, and you'll work faster." I allowed myself to be comforted and convinced, and after taking the other tests, left LA for home in Irvine feeling exhausted but relieved.

I completed my application for the Department of Molecular Biology at UCI by the January 31 deadline and was fairly confident that despite my GRE debacle, my good grades from UCT would carry the day. To be fully prepared for graduate school, I spent hours in the library brushing up on basic calculus, physics, and chemistry because I would need to take thermodynamics, kinetics, and quantum chemistry in the first year and would therefore need to know that background material. Georges gave me sample problems to work on the days he would be home late, and I was happy solving these, feeling within my comfort zone. I was excited when the envelope arrived from the Department of Molecular Biology. But then, I opened it and read, "Dear Miss Belfort, we regret to inform you we are unable to accommodate you in our incoming PhD class for the Fall semester. If you wish to be considered for the master's program, you will need to…" I couldn't read any further. My eyes welled with tears and my head began to pound. Rejected! An abject failure! I started to think of my mom, who always taught me each loss is an opportunity. Maybe this would be the time to give up and have a baby?

I brought this up with Georges, but he said, and I saw his point, that it was a bit early to have babies so soon after marriage at only twenty-three and I shouldn't give up on the PhD. He suggested I contact the head of graduate admissions at the Molecular Biology program, an assistant professor named Dr. Lee Hartwell, to make my case. So, that's what I did, trembling as I walked into Hartwell's office. He was surprised I spoke fluent English and explained that being from Africa and having a thirty-sixth-percentile score in the general GRE (I performed much better in the analytical and very well in biology), they couldn't possibly admit me into the department. Besides, my UCT grades were "only average," with mainly Bs and a few As. Fighting back the tears, I explained that I was clueless about the strategy for taking the GREs and those grades were actually very good in the context of the South African system. When he realized I was quite articulate and smart, he reread my letters of recommendation and said, "Okay, Marlene, although I can't reverse a unanimous decision of the Admissions Committee, I can put you on the waiting list and discuss your case at the next committee meeting." We shook hands, and I walked back home to Verano Place. The wait-list news gave me some hope, but then I thought of all those smart-as-a-whip American kids who were likely ahead of me on the list. Imposter syndrome loomed large.

A few weeks later, however, Dr. Hartwell called to say that one of their incoming students had turned them down, and I had been conditionally accepted into the Molecular Biology graduate program! I was a basket case of excitement and trepidation but soon settled into the lab of Dr. Daniel Wulff, working in bacterial genetics. Meanwhile, Dr. Hartwell, in his role as chair of graduate admissions, kept an eye on me, wanting to make absolutely sure he had made the right decision when he admitted me into the program. Eventually, Dr. Hartwell moved on from Irvine to Seattle, where he eventually became the head of the Fred Hutchinson Cancer Center and was awarded the Nobel Prize for work he'd done at UCI on the cell cycle. Then, almost comically, thirty years after Dr. Hartwell took a chance on me at UCI, he invited me to serve on the advisory board of "the Hutch," which I did for twelve years. I like to think this was his way of telling me he had no regrets about reversing the decision to accept me into the graduate program.

Back in the UCI years, our first baby, David, was born midway through my PhD program. I cherished little David, loved my work in bacterial genetics, and published my thesis work in four first-author publications, where Dr. Wulff was my only coauthor. All that in four years. I'm breathless just thinking back on that time. Those were happy years for Georges and me. We loved being parents and relished our work. We also enjoyed socializing with students on campus and dancing to the music of Janis Joplin and Jimi Hendrix, who were both taken from us too soon.

While I was cruising through my thesis work, my bench mate in the lab was a graduate student named Jim from Wyoming, whose work was progressing slowly. Jim told me I was the first Jew he had met and that I "lived up to expectations." The statement was not meant as a compliment, to be sure. That was my first brush with anti-Semitism given that in Cape Town, I had been totally insulated by the majority-Jewish community in which I had lived. I interpreted Jim's jab as coming from a place of competitiveness and insecurity.

But I paid him no mind. I loved the work and had developed a fascination with RNA, which would later become my specialty. In fact, it was when I was giving birth to David in 1970 at Hoag Memorial Hospital in Newport Beach, literally while I was in labor, with Georges and a nurse by my side, that I happened to read a *Nature* article about the independent discovery of the enzyme reverse transcriptase by David Baltimore and Howard Temin.[4] I remember turning to Georges and telling him excitedly about what I had just read, how RNA was capable of being transcribed backward into DNA. All he heard, however, was "going backward!" My delivery went just fine, as it turned out. But Georges needed to be treated for what he described as an excruciating headache at the thought of his baby going backward! This all came full circle when in 2010, I was invited by the National Academy of Sciences to organize a colloquium on the topic "Reverse transcriptase that shaped genomes." The event was held, coincidentally, at the Academy's west coast facility on the UCI campus to commemorate the fortieth anniversary of the discovery of reverse transcriptase. David Baltimore, who had since been awarded the Nobel Prize, agreed to be our keynote speaker. I introduced Dr. Baltimore's talk by telling the audience it was also the fortieth birthday of my oldest son, also a David, and recounting the "going backward" story, which had the audience and the Nobel winner laughing out loud. By that time, my career was on track, although the path had been anything but smooth.

---

[4] "Central Dogma Reversed," *Nature* 226 (1970): 1198–1199, https://doi.org/10.1038/2261198a0.

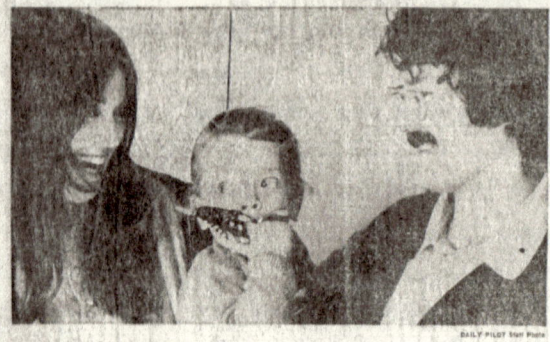

US CITIZEN, 1971: In California, I started graduate school at UCI—and also became a mom. Our firstborn, David, was eighteen months old when the local paper ran this piece about me becoming the first naturalized citizen of the newly incorporated city of Irvine.

Back in the early 1970s, I still needed all the help I could get. Thankfully, while we were living in Irvine, we were fortunate enough to have Georges's Uncle Semon and Aunt Annette close by in Newport Beach. Although not parental substitutes, they were very kind to us, and it was good to have family around. They loved our baby and often had us over for meals. Meanwhile, we both worked extremely hard at the lab and at taking care of our little David, for whom we hired a student nannie, Jannie Maxwell. Jannie took care of David as if he were her own, growing organic fruits and vegetables to feed him and assuaging some of our guilt over spending long hours away from him in the lab. I became a naturalized US citizen in the newly incorporated city of Irvine and worked hard at my research on a bacterial virus called phage lambda. Meanwhile, Georges was successful in his graduate studies, working on the theory of water structure at the Department of Sanitary Engineering. He had wanted to study chemical engineering, but that discipline didn't exist yet at UCI. I remember one of the engineering parties where a faculty wife learned that Georges was in Sanitary and asked him a technical question about the flush on her toilet. He was dumbfounded for a moment and then said, "Sorry, I can't help. I'm only a theoretical plumber." He got a good laugh with that one. I still call him my theoretical plumber.

We were in the first graduating class of PhDs at the UCI campus, with environmental activist and politician Ralph Nader as the keynote speaker at our commencement. We proudly received our diplomas, signed by the then-governor of California and head of the UC Board of Regents, none other than former actor and future president Ronald Reagan. Despite graduating with honors, I still felt something of an imposter. These feelings were tempered to a degree by my accomplishments, but I still couldn't get past the paucity of female graduate students and the fact that the molecular biology faculty at UCI was exclusively male—not a single woman in the twenty-person faculty to help me imagine what my future in science could look like.

The only female scientist in our department at UCI was Ethel Tessman, a glorified post-doc working as a research professor in her husband Irwin's lab. Ethel too had a son. We became close friends and maintained contact long after we left Irvine and the Tessmans moved to the University of Indiana. From our later mail correspondence (letters handwritten in tidy script) and occasional long-distance calls, it was clear Ethel was struggling. She had an acute sense of failure as a scientist and a mom. We visited the Tessmans in West Lafayette, but her mood was gloomy.

A few years later, while I was starting my career as an independent scientist, I received the shocking news that Ethel had taken her life by drinking cyanide from a shelf in the lab. Gone was a fellow female scientist, whose death brought me right back to my father's suicide. It also struck at the heart of my own vulnerability. I felt sad and wobbly but then recalled my mother and Oma, the rocks who kept our family grounded in South Africa. So, I continued to model myself after Mom, who had provided crucial support to our family as sole breadwinner after Dad died, fueling in me an unusual assumption that work *and* domestic investment were just, well, what women do. Or was it just us Sterns? Either way, I needed to motor on.

CHAPTER SEVEN

A SUPPORTIVE ENVIRONMENT FOR WORKING WOMEN— IMAGINE THAT!

The job market was tight in the US in the early 1970s, so after receiving our PhDs from UCI, Georges and I decided on a stint at the Hebrew University in Jerusalem for his first faculty position and my first post-doctoral experience. When we arrived in Israel, our university apartment was not yet ready for us and we had very limited funds, so Georges, two-year-old David, and I moved into government-subsidized housing in an indigent neighborhood called Katamon Tet. There, we lived with Russian and Moroccan immigrant families without a common language, and we shivered through the winter on stone floors with only a single kerosene heater. It was so frigid that to keep warm, we lined our lightweight clothes from Cape Town and California with David's terry-cloth diapers. We had no real winter clothes and couldn't afford new wardrobes as our salaries were low and we were already sending money to Georges's mom, Sophie, in Cape Town.

Naturally, it was a relief in many ways when we got to move, several months later, from Katamon Tet into faculty housing in Neve Sha'anan, a lovely neighborhood in Jerusalem. By this time, Georges had begun work in the School of Engineering, and I had returned to science after a brief stint at an "ulpan" (pronounced oel-pun), a Hebrew-language school for immigrants. We lived close to the "Knesset" (parliament), between the Israel Museum and the university's Givat Ram campus and within easy walking distance to both. The museum is a glorious place, home to the two-thousand-year-old Dead Sea Scrolls housed in the humidity-controlled Shrine of the Book. It also boasts an outdoor sculpture garden featuring works by Maillol, Moore, Picasso, and Rodin. And though our Israel adventure had a bit of a rough start, we soon found ourselves flourishing, befriending like-minded academic faculty in our new apartment building. We also visited relatives of my stepfather, the Rabbi, who embraced us. They were mainly "dahtiim" (devout people) and politically to the right, except for two women with whom we grew particularly close who defied religious norms and were politically left leaning. But in general, their entire large family of seven children and many grandchildren were extremely kind to us.

I started my post-doctoral studies with Dr. Amos Oppenheim at Hadassah Medical School, working on the same virus I had worked on as a graduate student in California: bacteriophage lambda, which infects bacterial cells. Although the scientific transition was smooth for me, only a few months after moving to Neve Sha'anan in the fall of 1973, the Yom Kippur War broke out, sending us to bomb shelters and causing us to fear for our lives. The Syrians invaded Israel from the north with tanks that greatly outnumbered those the Israelis had while the Egyptians crossed the Suez Canal in the south with great force. We were thunderstruck and terrified. Although both fronts were somewhat remote from Jerusalem, the war was no theoretical threat: A Katyusha rocket, with its terrifying sound, landed right next to our apartment building, blasting a huge crater into the ground.

Whenever we heard the dreaded air-raid sirens, we'd race down to the basement bomb shelter. Being in a dismal, damp, smelly, concrete, bomb-proof room with an active three-year-old is no one's idea of fun, but there were toys down there, and the children from the apartment building played together for hours on end in the dim light, oblivious to the miserable conditions—and their mothers' worst fears. The adults, mainly faculty wives, sat on uncovered mattresses on the rough, cold concrete floor. Most of the women's husbands were away fighting on the front lines. We comforted one another as we chatted and listened to the news on transistor radios. The reception was muffled in the shelter, and we could barely hear voices above the crackling. Although my spoken Hebrew is fairly fluent, it's not strong enough to get the finer nuances of a barely audible newscast, so I relied on friends for translation. But even I recognized the siren sound that signaled we could finally return to our apartments. With joyful relief, we'd carry our babies and toddlers out into the desperately needed fresh air and then race upstairs to our homes.

Georges could not serve in the army, not being an Israeli citizen, so he contributed to the war effort by driving a small classical music troupe of US volunteers to the front lines to entertain the active-service soldiers. Israel's very survival was at stake, so their victory in less than three weeks felt extremely liberating, and the ensuing peace agreement negotiated at Camp David between the presidents of Egypt, Israel, and the US—Anwar Sadat, Menachem Begin, and Jimmy Carter—was welcomed across the globe. As I was writing this book, on October 6, 2023, I said to Georges, "D'you know, it's fifty years today since the Yom Kippur War?" "Yeah," he said. "Amazing how we were so caught by surprise." Little did we know that the very next day, Hamas would invade southern Israel, killing 1,200 people and taking more than two hundred hostages, or that this would drag out into a long and horrible war in Gaza.

The more things change, the more they stay the same, I suppose. But one good thing that hasn't changed is the supportive environment for working mothers in Israel, which is a more child-centric country than any other I've lived in. From the cradle, children are revered, supported, and nurtured in profoundly caring ways, including being provided with universal healthcare and beautifully run nursery schools and day care centers. Even pregnant women are unusually revered.

Riding the bus to work every day, I always needed to scramble for a seat—that is, until I became visibly pregnant again. Then, someone would immediately stand up to offer me their place. Even childbirth was a wholesome experience. David's birth in California was a very clinical, sterile event. They wheeled me into the hospital in a chair, and a crew-cut, astronaut-like obstetrician immediately wanted to medicate me, which I resisted, having had Lamaze training. In contrast, when our next two sons, Gabriel (Gabi) and Jonathan (Yona), were born at Hadassah Hospital in Jerusalem, I walked from the lab in the medical school where I worked to a birthing room, where encouraging midwives helped me deliver naturally. My obstetrician was on hand during the births, but only in case some extraordinary intervention was required. Then, after birth, there was a robust support system to help new moms care for themselves and their babies and to look after and educate small children. This supportive environment, which allowed most Israeli mothers to work outside the home, had a profound impact on my confidence in combining my scientific career with parenting.

JERUSALEM, 1976: Our family grew to five in Jerusalem, where I was a post-doc at the Hebrew University and Georges, pictured here with our three sons, held a faculty position.

Unfortunately, my relationship with Amos, my post-doc mentor, was erratic. He had wild mood swings, and his approval of me was subject to his highs and lows. Also, his wife, who did great research with him, created tension in the lab and made me feel like an outsider. I worked as hard and creatively as I could, but my productivity was limited by having three small children. So, I used the joy I felt raising them with Georges to fill the void where satisfaction in the lab would have gone.

But finances and the constant threat of war took their toll. Fruits and vegetables are plentiful in Israel, and we ate lots of those, but for high protein, we could only afford chicken, milk products, eggs, and hummus. Toward the end of the month, we were usually down to just eggs and hummus. When the war caused blackouts and the chicken coops were dark, even eggs became scarce because stimulating the hens' endocrine systems with artificial light was forbidden. But we managed to make do, and I was grateful to be able to afford the "mitapellet" (nanny) who helped us care for the children. Occasionally, my mom sent us a bailout from Cape Town that allowed us to reach the end of the month more comfortably. It certainly didn't help our finances, though, when Georges went on jaunts to work in Europe and brought back expensive gifts for the children and me, inevitably leading to us scraping by on just hummus again. That made me angry. I didn't need expensive gifts; I needed the basic necessities for myself and the children.

On a happier note, we became close friends with a wonderful couple who were our neighbors in Neve Sha'anan, Aliza Dror and her husband Emmanuel Farjoun, a psychologist and mathematician, respectively. They were unusual in their anti-Zionist political persuasion. They were raised on a left-leaning "kibbutz" (communal farm) and often protested in favor of Israeli Arab rights. Their daughter Na'ama, a close friend of our son David, eventually married an Arab man from the town of Jericho. In part through this friendship and in part due to our anti-Apartheid values, we are sympathetic to the Palestinian cause to this day. But, of course, we simultaneously hold in our hearts an extraordinarily deep reverence for Israel as a Jewish homeland necessitated by the persecution of the Jewish diaspora, most notably during the Holocaust.

However, despite our love of the country and for our close Israeli friends and relatives, including the Rabbi's Israeli nieces and nephews and their children, the truth was we were tired of struggling to make ends meet. Also, frankly, I was afraid for the lives of our three sons since all three would need to serve in the Israeli army if we stayed. Georges was less fearful, maybe because that's just the way he is or perhaps he's more committed to the Israeli cause than I. Regardless, with a good deal of sadness and a heavy conscience, we decided to return to the US.

Initially, we failed to find anything suitable in our transcontinental job search, so in 1977, both Georges and I took temporary, one-year positions at Northwestern University in the Chicago area. We assumed this situation, and in particular being in the US instead of applying from abroad, would help us more readily find permanent positions in the US. All five of us flew from Israel to Chicago together. David and Gabi were fully bilingual in Hebrew and English, but Yona, who was just two, knew only Hebrew, the language he spoke to our mitapellet. Georges worked as a visiting professor, and I did my second post-doc, also on phage, on the Evanston campus. We rented a tiny house in a Jewish neighborhood on Chicago's north side, in West Rogers Park. The children were happy, David at a Hebrew day school in Skokie and Gabi and Yona at a welcoming neighborhood day care center, which somewhat assuaged my angst over dragging them around the world.

Next, it was time to apply for "real" positions in the US. We were eventually presented with two solutions to the two-body problem. The first was offers from Northwestern for me to work at the Medical School in downtown Chicago and Georges to teach in Evanston. The second opportunity was in the Capital District of Upstate New York, where Georges would teach at Rensselaer Polytechnic Institute (RPI) in Troy and I was offered a position at the research and testing labs of the New York State Department of Health, later known as Wadsworth

Center, in Albany. Although we favored the Northwestern jobs, they were about twenty miles apart linked by congested Chicago roads in prime real-estate areas. Given our finances, we couldn't figure out a way to find affordable housing and make the shuttling back and forth work for us and the children. I was unable to reconcile Yona's needs, given his language difficulty and tender age, with the demands of an urban commute. Also, I didn't want to stop breastfeeding until we were more settled.

So, we accepted the jobs in New York in 1978, convinced this was an easier place to raise a family. We planned on staying a few years and moving on when the children were a little older. Four decades later, we were still there.

CHAPTER EIGHT

A STRUGGLE AND THE BIG BREAKTHROUGH

We liked the cultural spillover from New York City and Boston into Albany and also its proximity to Montreal. With a little help from my mom, we purchased our dream house on six acres of land in a bedroom community of Albany called Slingerlands. The house had no street number, only a name: Playfields. It was an unusual single-story house with a flat roof built on a slab (no basement as is customary for houses in the Northeast), with wood-paneled walls, an open living area with skylights, and large windows stretching almost floor to ceiling. It was a Frank Lloyd Wright kind of place. Neighbors were hidden from sight by the large lot and trees. The windows, overlooking grassland and woods, brought the outside indoors, and we watched the seasons change, from riotous color in the fall to snowscapes in the winter through a muddy, blossom-laden spring and the glorious green of summer, from the comfort of our living room. I could see outside from the kitchen, watching the children play soccer as I cooked. It was a beautiful place for us to live and grow as a family.

We lived at Playfields for forty-two years as our careers advanced and the boys matured, went off to college, and married. Georges began as an assistant professor and proceeded more-or-less linearly to eventually becoming an endowed institute professor at RPI, the highest academic position possible. I, on the other hand, proceeded in fits and starts, accepting the tenure-track research position because it had no teaching obligation and I thought it might be a better fit with the children than a faculty position. But I didn't understand the lack of freedom to pursue my own research inherent in the position and came precariously close to being fired. Eventually, despite a research career beyond my wildest dreams at Wadsworth Center, I needed to leave because of poor research support. I joined the Department of Biological Sciences at the University at Albany (UAlbany) in 2011 and remain there to this day.

Our three boys were approaching nine, five, and three years of age when we purchased the house in Slingerlands. This was home, so I felt I could finally stop nursing our youngest, Yona, despite his protests and attempts to unbutton my blouses. The boys thrived in their new home. They were rambunctious but good-natured boys; they had their battles but also laughed a lot together, with David acting as the ringleader. They enjoyed their day care center, Pierce Hall on the downtown SUNY campus, and schools, the Hebrew Academy then the neighborhood public schools. Soon, they became deeply involved in sports, and a soccer field and basketball hoop were installed in the backyard. Neighborhood children came over to play, and Georges joined right in as their coach. I was constantly surrounded by sweaty, noisy boys. It was like living in a men's locker room. But I was pleased to have them adapting so well to our new environment and engaged in healthy activities as I ran the household, cooked, shopped, managed our finances, arranged for childcare, and juggled my research position.

Yona, today a father in his own right, describes Playfields as part playground for the neighborhood, part hostel for visitors from around the world, part party house, and part shared workspace. It was a place where relatives, friends, neighbors, and colleagues were all welcome; that was both the South African and Israeli style, to have people visit informally and stay as the need arose. One night, Gabi ran into a German guest of Georges's on his way to the bathroom and asked, "Who are you? Do my parents know you're here?" Hosting houseguests was so routine for my family, he didn't balk at running into a stranger in his own home.

I have spoken with our adult children about how our being scientists might have influenced them. Yona, an engineer and product designer by profession, told me he learned to follow his passion rather than chase money and that his exposure to wildly successful people was helpful as he pursued his own ambitions. As an eight-year-old, Yona met Nobel laureate James Watson, then the director of Cold Spring Harbor Laboratory, and Jim seemed to him like a regular goofy guy wearing red slacks. Such encounters provided Yona the confidence to engage with anyone. When I asked if he ever felt neglected by me, Yona replied, "That's pure bullshit, Mom. Besides, I could always lean on Dad or my brothers." Our sons still lean on each other pretty routinely.

Gabi, the MD–PhD, believes our directness and truthfulness with them as children stemmed from our being scientists who cherished facts (more on that in the final chapter). "I never felt my childhood was governed by impenetrable tradition. I always felt my mom and dad had reasons for the way they raised us. Of course, we challenged them, but when we did, we knew we needed a sound counterargument." Gabi indeed challenged us plenty, mainly with boyish naughtiness, though that could more than test our parenting abilities.

David, the employment attorney and lone non-scientist/engineer, married a physician–scientist and personally embraces technology. He also loves representing discrimination clients and "righting the wrongs of bias because of the value you two imparted, but even handling company employment issues and navigating the logic of the law is an academic exercise I enjoy." I find it amusing that he relishes working with academics, scientists, doctors, and engineers as clients because he perceives us as living in an ivory tower, lacking any business sense and "naive about real life." Ah, well. David claims, "Striving to kick ass is what we do—we are all very competitive in our own way, but always with an eye on doing good." "Doing good" brings to mind the words of author/photographer Carolyn Jones, "I learned that whether or not we work our children are influenced by the kind of women we are. If they see us helping others they will grow up caring. If they see us fulfilling our dreams they will grow up having dreams. If we cherish them as children they will cherish their own children."[5]

Back in those early days in Albany, I took my different responsibilities mostly in stride, but pretty soon, life became difficult for me at Wadsworth. Not only did I feel guilty for leaving the children to work long days and not being there to greet them with fresh-baked cookies as soon as they arrived home from school, as other neighborhood moms seemed to be, but my work felt like a job in a state bureaucracy rather than a place where I was free to pursue my own research and grow scientifically. My immediate supervisor and the lab chief of biochemistry Dr. Frank Maley was an excellent, old-school biochemist, but he had me reporting to his wife, Dr. Gladys Maley, who was a classical protein chemist, fifteen years older than I, and uncomfortable with my more-modern training.

One would think after my Jerusalem experience, I would have been more cautious about working for another husband–wife team. I always felt the spousal relationship dominated the workplace, creating a power axis that made healthy, one-on-one interactions between me and either spouse difficult. While working for the Maleys, instead of speaking up in a positive, healthy way and trying to address the regrettable dynamic, for the most part, I just stewed in silent frustration. I also threw myself into child-rearing and household duties. If I couldn't find satisfaction at work, I told myself, I would find it at home as a counterbalance to my professional unhappiness. I'd start each day by folding laundry, imagining the strong bodies of our growing children as I stroked their clothes flat and sorted them into neat piles. Folding laundry generated the satisfaction of small accomplishments, which

---

[5] Todd Lyon and Carolyn Jones, *The Family of Women: Voices Across the Generations* (Abbeville Press, 1999), 11.

steadied me. Finding unpaired socks didn't matter. What the children left in their pants pockets often provided interesting distractions, like Twinkie wrappers that made me angry because I tried so hard to pack healthy lunches. Or, in their advanced teenage years, a condom that had me a bit concerned and very curious.

It felt like I was in control and fulfilled as I was doing the laundry. But often, after I got to work, all hell broke loose, and Gladys would criticize my work as I struggled to perform biochemical experiments on the active site of an enzyme, called "thymidylate synthase." I was trained as a molecular biologist and geneticist, so learning biochemistry was challenging. A friend from UCI, Ethel Tessman, before she passed, advised me, "Take biochemistry like it's medication; it will make you better." I tried to find strength in her words but often still needed to have a good cry in the women's room. Then, I'd go back home to Georges and the boys, my head throbbing, and feel enveloped by their love and *their* healthy needs, which displaced my own as I shifted gears to take care of them and prepare dinner.

No matter how out of control life seemed, we ate together as a family whenever possible. I loved to cook for Georges and the boys, who were all healthy eaters. They would play in the backyard until I rang an old, rusty cowbell, which was their signal to come in for dinner.

That cowbell is still in use today, but Yona is the one ringing it now to summon *his* boys in from playing outside.

Around the dinner table, we would chat about our day as the boys squabbled over who received the biggest portion. Then, Georges would wash the dishes, and the children would perform their prescribed chores, like taking out the trash or wiping down the kitchen counters, whining all the way. I would try to pay serious attention to their various needs for a brief period every evening. After some post-dinner activities, like watching TV (thirty minutes only!) or playing Ping-Pong (table tennis), Georges and I would lie down with the children and read to them, at which point my physical and emotional exhaustion would invariably take over, and I'd fall asleep on one of their beds.

Then, one day, in the midst of this daily work/home grind, I got what seemed like some unexpected, good news from Wadsworth. Frank called me to his office to tell me he would sponsor a trip for me to travel to New Orleans to present my work on the catalytic center of thymidylate synthase at an American Society for Biochemistry and Molecular Biology (ASBMB) meeting. That was a rare thrilling moment for me at work, but it was all too brief. He then sternly informed me that after the conference and once I had sent out our enzyme work for publication, he was likely to terminate me before the tenure decision. He advised me to look around for another job and proceeded to register his complaints with my somewhat variable work schedule (to accommodate the needs of the family, of course), even accusing me of falsifying my time card. Thud! Had I really done something wrong or was he just trying to get rid of me? I was confused and thoroughly deflated. How could he possibly allege time card irregularities when I worked such long hours? Who cared when I arrived and left if I got the job done? And now what was I supposed to do? How could I find another research position locally? Was I really being faced with possibly having to relocate our family yet again?

I gritted my teeth and went to New Orleans to present the poster at the ASBMB meeting, doing all I could to hold myself together.[6] The work was well received. To unwind after the poster session, I went for a walk on bustling Bourbon Street, where I ran into two former UCI professors, Cal McLaughlin and Kivie Moldave, who were also attending the ASBMB meeting. They were excited to see me but quickly became dismayed as I responded to their query of how I was doing with, "Terribly! I'm in the process of being fired!" "How could that possibly be?" they asked. "You were our most outstanding student in your graduating class." They tried to encourage me, but I was totally despondent at the prospect of finding a new job. Disheartened, I flew

---

6   Marlene Belfort, Gladys F. Maley, and Frank Maley, "A Single Functional Arginyl Residue Involved in the Catalysis Promoted by *Lactobacillus casei* Thymidylate Synthetase," *Archives of Biochemistry and Biophysics* 204, vol. 1 (October 1980): 340–349, https://doi.org/10.1016/0003-9861(80)90042-9.

back to Albany and back to my routine, part of which was trying to absorb some of my pain in the comfort of our cohesive family unit. But we were all terribly unsettled by my impending termination.

A couple weeks later, Frank summoned me to his office again to tell me that Kivie Moldave, who was the editor in chief of an influential book series, *Methods in Enzymology*, had phoned him. On this call, apparently Kivie mentioned our New Orleans encounter and suggested Frank give me a chance to continue working on thymidylate synthase but using a molecular-genetic approach to complement the biochemistry he and Gladys were doing. Then, he turned to me and asked, "Are you willing to do that?" Of course, I was! There was huge potential to focus on thymidylate synthase function using our different approaches, and besides, setting up the genetic systems would take me well beyond the tenure consideration.

The rest is for the scientific history books. Given my experience with phage, I readily cloned the thymidylate synthase gene of phage T4 and then set up the new Sanger DNA sequencing technology in the lab.[7] Dr. Fred Chu, another research scientist in Frank's group, used the technology to sequence the T4 thymidylate synthase gene. However, when analyzing the results, Fred found an aberration in the sequence. By combining Gladys's expertise in protein chemistry with mine in genetics, we concluded the anomaly was an interruption in the coding sequence for thymidylate synthase, commonly called an "intervening sequence," or "intron." But bacteria and phage were widely viewed as not having introns.

We had made a serendipitous and important discovery. For me this was a eureka moment—finding an intron in a lower life form that would link evolutionarily primitive organisms to more sophisticated ones, with implications for the very origin of life on earth! I experienced chills from the enormous thrill of discovery, feeling excited and triumphant about seeing further than anyone had seen before.

---

7   Frederick Sanger, S. Nicklen, and A. R. Coulson, "DNA Sequencing with Chain-Terminating Inhibitors," *PNAS* 74, no. 12 (December 1977): 5463–5467, https://doi.org/10.1073/pnas.74.12.5463.

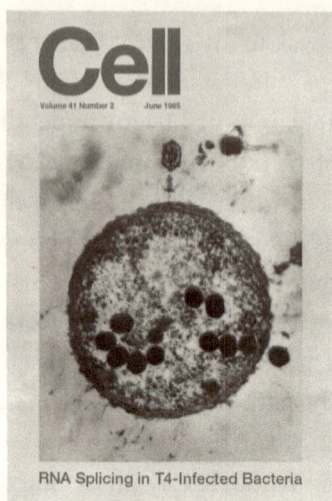

COVER OF *CELL*, 1985, VOL. 41 (2):
After moving to New York state in the late '70s and while working at the Wadsworth Center, the Maleys, Fred Chu, and I discovered RNA splicing in phage T4-infected bacteria, publishing two high-profile papers, including this one in *Cell*. With permission from Elsevier Press.

We published two high-profile papers, one in the *Proceedings of the National Academy of Sciences of the United States of America* (PNAS) in 1984 on the existence of an intervening sequence in the thymidylate synthase gene of phage T4 and another a year later in *Cell* showing that cutting out of the intron and joining the external sequences in a process called "splicing" is at the level of the RNA.[8] These papers caused a big splash and were widely editorialized, not only because they represented a first but also because they had implications for the origin of life and practical uses in biotechnology.[9] That was the real beginning of my life in the field of RNA science.

---

8   Frederick Chu et al., "Intervening Sequence in the Thymidylate Synthase Gene of Bacteriophage T4," *PNAS* 81, no. 10 (May 1984): 3049–3053, https://doi.org/10.1073/pnas.81.10.304.

9   Marlene Belfort et al., "Processing of the Intron-Containing Thymidylate Synthase (td) Gene of Phage T4 Is at the RNA Level," *Cell* 41, no. 2 (June 1985): 375–382, https://doi.org/10.1016/s0092-8674(85)80010-6.

CHAPTER NINE

THE CURSE AND THE BLESSING OF THE SUCCESSFUL FEMALE SCIENTIST

One might guess the Maleys and Fred would be overjoyed, beside themselves with excitement and gratification over our discovery and publication in prestigious journals, but instead, the opposite was true. They felt I had received undue recognition for our breakthrough and was stealing the limelight. Our professional relationship grew very tense, but we continued to publish prolifically until out of the blue, in 1985, Frank handed me a performance evaluation filled with criticism that ranked me "Effective but Needs Substantial Improvement," which, according to the fine print on the form, indicated, "The employee meets performance expectations only at a minimum. Some tasks may require extra direction by the supervisor, or the supervisor may find it necessary to avoid assigning tasks to the employee." His other options were to rank me "Outstanding," "Highly Effective," or "Effective" on the one hand or "Unsatisfactory" on the other.

The evaluation was signed by Frank but not his supervisor, Dr.

Herbert Dickerman, the deputy director of the center, who refused to attach his name to the document. Herb knew full well I was the one who led the group out of obscurity and into the scientific spotlight while securing independent funding for my lab from both the National Science Foundation (NSF) and the National Institutes of Health (NIH). But the writing was on the wall: Clearly, Frank was creating a paper trail to fire me for insubordination given that the criticisms were not about my work but about my acting independently. He accused me of recruiting graduate students without sufficient consultation, performing experiments without his knowledge or permission, and collaborating without "the supervisor's consent."

In desperation, I discussed the evaluation with my colleagues and the director of the Wadsworth Center, Herb's boss. A huge brouhaha ensued, and to cut a very long and extremely painful story short, I had several advocates who rallied on my behalf. The center director, rather than face a public outcry and possible lawsuit, decided to remove me from Frank's supervision and place me in a different unit headed by Dr. Lorraine (Lori) Flaherty, who was one of my supporters in my battle against Frank. In a nutshell, she granted me complete scientific independence and encouraged my further success.

That all happened forty years ago, but I've never quite been able to shake it and have long wondered what really provoked the treatment I received. Yes, lab politics are real, and all the pressure and competition can and often does lead to some ugliness. Anyone pursuing a career in science needs to be aware of this reality. The life of a scientist is not always fun or pleasant or even rewarding. Like all careers, there are times when the lofty ideals that draw people to the sciences in the first place—including humility and a commitment to empiricism over ego, truth finding over credit hoarding—can feel in short supply. Staying clear eyed and prepared for interpersonal conflict are imperative to succeeding in a scientific career, and I've chosen to spend so much time on this particular story from my past to illustrate how important they are. This story carries valuable lessons about the importance of people skills and emotional intelligence, which were certainly not prioritized when I was a student but are now integral to a STEM (Science, Technology, Engineering, and Math) education, as they should be.

RNA CATALYSIS SPLICING EVOLUTION, 1988: This extraordinary conference organized by David Shub and myself launched our careers in the RNA world. **Front:** M. Green, S. Wessler, M. Belfort, G. Bruening, D. Shub, P. Perlman; **Middle:** S. Altman, H. Robertson, A. Weiner, J. Boothroyd, N. Maizels, F. Michel, P, Sharp; **Top:** B. Dujon, J. Belote, T. Cech, C. Guthrie, O. Uhlenbeck, N. Pace, J. Abelson.[10]

Maybe those of us who came up in that era were just less equipped to deal with things like the inevitable friction in scientific labs, which are populated, after all, by regular, messy human beings. But can that really explain why the Maleys seemed to have it in for me? At the time, my sample size was small, but having now observed many labs, I know it was certainly out of the norm to document their displeasure so pointedly. Were their actions based on jealousy? Or insecurity? Or were their allegations gendered? At the time, that last thought would not have occurred to me. Probably because of the experience of going

---

10   Marlene Belfort and David A. Shub, *RNA: Catalysis, Splicing, Evolution* (Elsevier Press: 1989).

to an all-girls school and being desensitized to bias against women. But knowing what I know today of workplace discrimination, it's hard to imagine there wasn't some gender component to the "stealing the limelight" accusation and all the resentment that seemed to lie behind it. Would a male have been criticized for his ambition or striving for success after leading a group from obscurity to prominence?

Whatever the case may be, it was all behind me now. My career soared. Under Lori Flaherty, we discovered the introns that Fred had shown can self-splice—that is, behave as catalytic RNA enzymes—can also behave as mobile genetic elements, moving from one place to another on DNA genomes. The implications of these findings for genome evolution became obvious to us, and we published papers in *Cell*, *Nature*, and *Science*, the most renowned scientific journals in the world. My colleague at UAlbany David Shub and I worked together on the discovery of more introns in phage and organized an international meeting titled "RNA: Catalysis, Splicing, Evolution." Of the twenty-five or so speakers we invited from around Europe and the US, about half were eventually elected to the prestigious US National Academy of Sciences and four went on to win Nobel Prizes. I felt heartened by the conference's success and found myself comfortable in the world of RNA scientists.

My time at Wadsworth may have had a traumatic beginning, but the world truly became my oyster when Lori was assigned as my lab chief. She gave me strong support and friendship, and my lab grew from strength to strength, recruiting post-docs from around the globe, attracting copious research dollars from several funding agencies, and publishing in the highest-quality journals. I was invited to serve on international science boards, grant panels, editorial boards, and advisory bodies.

My administrative responsibilities began thirteen years into my time at Wadsworth in 1991, when I was appointed associate director of the Molecular Genetics Program, which was directed by Lori, who mentored me. The following year, the director of the Wadsworth, Dr. Lawrence (Larry) Sturman, invited me to lead a new facility, the Axelrod Institute, which involved hiring about a dozen research scientists, mostly molecular geneticists. In 1994, he promoted me again, making me director of the Division of Genetic Disorders, a position I held for fourteen years. This division included the same junior researchers I had hired, whom I enjoyed mentoring, plus Lori's whole lab (Lori was now reporting to me) and people from the Newborn Screening Program of New York State, roughly 250 staff total. I enjoyed it all: the administrative work; reporting to Larry, whose brilliance I admired; and being supported by both administrative office staff and a talented lab manager. The substantial support allowed me to continue my research, and I was invited to present our work on national and international stages.

THE GOOD OLD DAYS AT WADSWORTH CENTER, 1995: Lori Flaherty (left), my mentor and friend, and Larry Sturman (right), the Wadsworth Center director, hosted a seminar visit by Shirley Tilghman, the soon-to-be-president of Princeton University.

In 1994, I was elected to the American Academy of Arts and Sciences and in 1999 to the American Academy of Microbiology and the National Academy of Sciences. The National Academy of Sciences, imagine that! The Academy was then a bastion of elite, male scientists, a boys' club, whose members I admired and revered, almost feared. At the time, less than one in ten Academy members were women. By now, that ratio has probably doubled. After I processed the reality that this girl from the tip of Africa had been admitted to one of the world's most selective scientific societies, I was elated and infused with a sense of purpose: to use my elevated platform to be a role model for young women and promote other deserving scientists.

INDUCTION INTO THE NATIONAL ACADEMY OF SCIENCES, 2000: In the 1990s, my career soared at Wadsworth Center, and I was elected to a number of prestigious organizations, including the National Academy of Sciences, where less than one in ten members at the time were women. Here, I am shown at the National Academy of Sciences in Washington, DC, with Bruce Alberts, then president of the organization, on the left.

My single female role model as a developing scientist in the RNA field, and advocate for me, was Joan Steitz. Joan is five years my elder, has been at Yale for more than fifty years, and is a leader in RNA science as well as a member of many academies and the recipient of accolades too numerous to count. Joan would send talented, Yale-trained PhDs my way as post-docs and nominate me for awards. My career certainly would not have progressed in the way it did without her. But it was also Joan who taught me, through both her words and actions, to support the next generation of women in science. And even though we're only five years apart, there were even fewer of us when Joan started on her scientific path. She told me recently that at the time I was in graduate school in 1969, she attended the Cold Spring Harbor Symposia on Quantitative Biology as one of three female speakers out of a hundred. She was really one of the true pioneers.

Having known Joan for so long, I began to think about how similar yet different our paths have been. Joan was without children when she spoke at the Cold Spring Harbor Symposia, just as I was beginning to have babies and believe I could indeed be a scientist and a mom. This conviction was reinforced when I lived in Israel, with help from its supportive government policies and family-first culture. And it was probably because of this burgeoning confidence that I could feel okay about motherhood taking center stage for me and filling my work-satisfaction void (that void I felt in Israel and during my initial years at Wadsworth). But when Joan stood at that podium in her late twenties, there was no question that, for her, science was front and center. At that time, the choice for most smart, ambitious women like Joan was binary: career or children, and I'm not sure she then saw or believed there could be another way. But now, in part because of the great work Joan and others have done to support women in science, there very much is.

Joan and I are both now in what I like to call the "fourth quarter" (see Part Five) of our lives, and these days, she is a proud grandma like me. But back when her son, Jonathan, born when Joan was in her late thirties, was a toddler, the Belfort boys were already much older, going into middle and high school. Then, before Georges and I knew it, the nest had begun to empty. We weren't immune to the usual parental sadness that accompanies the crossing of this threshold, the wistfulness over the passage of time and cycles of life. But we were also very excited for them. The boys were on their way to becoming themselves, to leading successful, independent lives. Meanwhile, my own professional life would continue on at Wadsworth, and though a mom never really stops being a mom, this designation was no longer "center stage," as it had once been.

HIGH SCHOOL GRADUATION, 1994: The youngest of our sons, Yona the graduate, before leaving the nest. Yona is flanked by his brothers, Dave and Gabi. The happy threesome remain very connected to each other to this day.

One amusing intersection between my now-grown children and my work occurred when I picked up the journal *Nature* and found a letter to the editor titled "Mother Knows Best." The letter, starting out *Sir-* [sic], pointed to some misinformation in *Nature* on the occurrence of introns and cited our original 1984 PNAS paper with me as senior author. The letter ended, "It's been a long time since I uttered these words, but I couldn't be more proud to say, 'Mommy told me so.'" It was signed "Gabriel M. Belfort." *My* Gabi!

Later, he and our other two sons all ended up living in Boston, prompting us to purchase a second home on Cape Cod to be closer to them. Our accountant told us not to spend more than $300,000, so Georges and I drove to the Cape one Saturday afternoon and looked at six houses, all under $300,000. At the end of the day, we told the realtor we'd take house number six. "You must be kidding," was her response. "People don't buy a house in an afternoon!" Not kidding. We had little time to be picky given we were consumed by our science and working as hard as ever. David and Gabi came out from Boston the next day (Yona was in graduate school in California at the time) and gave the house their thumbs-up. We signed the purchase and sales agreement the day after that. Over the years, we've renovated and added to our Cape house, which we call "Kaap Huisie" (Afrikaans for "little Cape house") and which continues to be a major hub for family gatherings. We've been on thousands of walks on neighborhood beaches along the shores of the same Atlantic Ocean, albeit 7,500 miles north, on which Georges and I first met and were raised. The same Atlantic Ocean that gobbled up my dad and took him away from me. There's a sad sweetness here.

Meanwhile, the boys matured and married. All three of their wives are highly impressive women, all three physicians. This last detail contributed to the title of this book. One day, when we were all together, one of our seven grandchildren, Strand, asked his mother, Erin, "Mommy, can boys also be doctors?" We all burst out laughing. Inside, I beamed.

By the way, all three daughters-in-law also mentor trainees and are involved in research. One can't help but wonder how my career focus played into our sons' mate selections.

But I digress. After being elected to the National Academy of Sciences, my lab continued to do good research at Wadsworth, which was in its heyday. A colleague, collaborator, and friend, Dr. Joachim Frank, became a prestigious Howard Hughes Medical Institute (HHMI) investigator, and the young molecular geneticists I had hired thrived. So, I was saddened when Larry told me he was preparing to step down as director of Wadsworth. "Would you consider the job?" he asked me. Absolutely not! There was no way I would sacrifice my research program, which taking the directorship would have required. "Who then?" asked Larry. We discussed two possibilities: one of the other four division directors or Jill Taylor, a competent virologist at the center. I thought it was worth taking a chance on Jill, and that's what Larry did. However, Jill was focused on the public health aspects of Wadsworth, and we did not see eye to eye about the importance of research. So, I found myself in another no-win situation, and it became clear things needed to change for me. I decided to step down from my position as division director. Whereas Jill and I seemed pitted against each other, Lori remained my staunchest advocate. Sadly, in 2006, Lori lost a long battle with cancer (I was by her side, holding her hand), and Joachim decided to move his lab to Columbia University. Other excellent researchers started to leave Wadsworth too. Not long after, Joachim was awarded the Nobel Prize in Chemistry for the work he did at Wadsworth. Of course, Columbia got the credit. Nevertheless, we were thrilled for him and proud that our own institution, Wadsworth, though less glamorous than the Ivy League where Joachim wound up, had produced Nobel-winning work.

MY RESEARCH GROUP AT WADSWORTH CENTER, 2001: The lab was a happy place and international hub, with trainees from Canada, China, England, Germany, Japan, Spain, and the US in this picture alone. I am sitting on the motorcycle of one of my post-docs.

My own lab at Wadsworth was a happy place, with a steady stream of wonderful students, post-docs, and technicians, three of whom stayed for twenty years and became my lab managers. But with time, it became obvious to me I needed to look for another job and move my operation elsewhere. Reflecting back on that decision from more than a decade ago, I'm reminded of the words from a recent graduation speech at the University of Pennsylvania by the PBS news journalist Amna Nawaz, who said, "Go where you are wanted, where you and your voice and your talents are needed...Welcome into your world the ones who will tell you the hard truths, not because they want to bring you down, but because they want to help you get where you're going."[11] Wonderfully sound advice from a wise young woman.

Fortuitously, Georges was at the same time being recruited to start a chemical engineering program at Duke, and we both received offers almost too good to refuse. I took the offer to Jill, still hoping we wouldn't need to move to North Carolina and farther from our children, two of whom now lived in the Boston area and the other in southern Maine, all within easy driving distance. But rather than counter the offer, Jill wished me luck. When my colleagues learned I was thinking of leaving, Arlene Ramsingh, an immunologist, rallied the troops, and several got together and petitioned Wadsworth to make a counteroffer to keep me there. They felt demoralized at the prospect of my leaving—but their appeal was to no avail. They told me they were devastated, and I felt bereft at abandoning them. When it became apparent I would definitely be leaving, the women scientists organized a lunch, at which the idea of forming the group Women of Wadsworth (WoW) was born. More about WoW in Chapter Eighteen.

Given there was no counteroffer from Wadsworth, Georges and I planned to move to Duke. Around this time, I went to a neighborhood baby shower and ran into UAlbany Arts and Sciences Dean Elga Wulfert. When she asked me how I was doing at Wadsworth, I told her not well and that I'd soon be leaving for Duke. She was flabbergasted that

---

11 Amna Nawaz, Commencement Address, University of Pennsylvania College of Arts and Sciences, May 15, 2022.

Wadsworth was letting me go and arranged an immediate meeting in her office, asking me to bring along the Duke offer letter, which I did.

Elga then countered Duke's offer, penny for penny, and threw in a light teaching load, and so in 2011, I moved my lab, grants, and team of about a dozen scientists from Wadsworth to UAlbany. Although Georges would have preferred a move to Duke, RPI was happy to keep him and gave him a nice salary increase. I have been treated kindly at UAlbany and am happy to bring recognition to the university by winning awards and serving on prominent advisory boards, like the NIH Council of Councils. At NIH, I served at the pleasure of the then-director, Dr. Francis Collins, sitting on the other side of the research funding barricade. While enjoying that service and impressed by Francis's smarts and charm, not to mention his guitar and motorcycle, I reflected on my decision to move to UAlbany with great satisfaction. One of the joys of the job was being a member of a newly launched RNA Institute, that draws in RNA researchers from around UAlbany to interact. A couple years after I landed there, I helped recruit an up-and-coming RNA scientist, Andy Berglund, as Institute director. Andy is a well respected and popular leader whose generosity of spirit pervades the place. It continues to feel good to be working there.

I sometimes wonder about my decision in favor of Albany over Northwestern in the early days and over Duke more recently. No question these were both choices predicated on family considerations—what was best for our children or proximity to our children. But was it also the imposter beginning to surface again? There may also have been a level of comfort for me in swimming in a small pond. I tend to like small ponds. The converse of that is discomfort with large ponds. A feeling of safety versus a tinge of insecurity.

For fourteen years now, I have been at UAlbany. For most of that time, I have served as the director of the Interdisciplinary Life Science Initiative, which is housed in a modern building that has labs from the Departments of Biology, Chemistry, Nanoscale Science and Engineering, Physics, and Psychology. It's a pleasure to be among the students and faculty interacting across disciplines. I feel validated and valued at UAlbany, and although it lacks the prestige of Duke, I am in easy driving distance of our children and grandchildren. For me, that matters. This situation provides another example of muddling through when things get messy and embracing the uncertainty, allowing it to percolate as preparation for the next step. In fact, that has become one of my fundamental principles in life: wallow in a professional problem or domestic dilemma until the path forward becomes clear and feels right. Doing what *feels* right and good rather than what *appears* best is my golden rule.

CHAPTER TEN

HELPING OTHERS SEE THE WIN–WIN

In a recent presentation to an RNA crowd, I was asked if I prefer the term "work–life integration" over the more commonly used "work–life balance." These terms have become hackneyed, and the focus on terminology has unfortunately led to a sense of fatigue among many. That's a pity because the fundamental ideas are very important. I find that both terms have merit, "integration" because my work and life are intertwined and "balance" because of the steadiness I feel straddling work and life. If I stood on only one leg and committed myself exclusively to research, I would lose my stability, as I would if I dedicated myself to parenting alone. Instead, I like to pursue a kind of dynamic equilibrium. Work–life "balance" is often criticized as a flawed goal, and therefore, I use the word "integration," despite my comfort with both terms. Regardless of what we call it, juggling career with a fulfilled domestic life, despite its great difficulties, as in my early Wadsworth Center days and as I will describe more generally later in this chapter, has been shown to be positively related to job and life satisfaction and negatively related to anxiety and depression across different cultures worldwide.[12]

Taking a step back now, about seven years into the empty nest, in 2001, with the three boys grown into men and well on their way to graduating from law (David), medical (Gabi), and engineering/design (Yona) graduate schools and starting to marry, I reflected on how caring for them grounded me and how all my scientific distractions (my guilt notwithstanding) afforded them the freedom to develop their independence. I wrote several articles on how parenting and scientific work can buttress each other. In a paper in *Current Biology* titled "The Win–Win Potential for Motherhood and Science," I argued that women who would like to become mothers should embrace, rather than fear, combining children with their careers. At the time, I wrote, "Although almost one-half of graduate students in the sciences are women, the number who are full professors, scientific leaders, or members in the National Academy of Sciences is in the 3 to 8 percent range."[13] I called these successful female scientists "the 5 percent," and as a member of this elite club and a fulfilled mom, I tried to encourage those considering both roles to go for it. I made the point that if they are willing to work hard, make sacrifices, and recruit help, undertaking both roles can make them better scientists and more balanced parents.

Shortly before her death, Supreme Court Justice Ruth Bader Ginsburg wrote an opinion piece in the *New York Times* in which she gave advice for living. She had two children and described combining her parenting role with her career as follows: "Each part of my life provided respite from the other and gave me a sense of proportion that classmates trained only on law studies lacked."[14] I couldn't agree more.

---

12 Jarrod M. Haar et al., "Outcomes of Work–Life Balance on Job Satisfaction, Life Satisfaction and Mental Health: A Study Across Seven Cultures,"*Journal of Vocational Behavior* 85, no. 3 (December 2014): 361–373, https://doi.org/10.1016/j.jvb.2014.08.010.

13 Marlene Belfort, "The Win–Win Potential for Motherhood and Science," *Current Biology* 11, no. 2 (January 2001): R41–42, https://doi.org/ 10.1016/S0960-9822(01)00005-7.

14 Ruth Bader Ginsburg, R, "Ruth Bader Ginsburg's Advice for Living," *New York Times*, opinion, October 2, 2016, https://www.nytimes.com/2016/10/02/opinion/Sunday/ruth-bader-ginsburgs-advice-for-living.html.

In fact, there are many unexpected advantages of juggling career and home for women and their families.[15] I found that life with children can work in synergy with life in the lab and vice versa, with transferable skills like communication, management, leadership, nurturing, and problem-solving featuring prominently in both the home and professional spheres. For example, parenting and mentoring draw on some of the same insights and instincts; dealing with children's shenanigans demands similar coping skills to responding to the antics of graduate students flailing around the lab. Creative cooking and original experimentation likewise rely on similar organizational prowess, inventiveness, divergent thinking, rulemaking, rule breaking, and risk-taking behaviors. Following recipes in my kitchen is as constraining as reading protocols in the lab; I would always be tempted to do things a little better or a bit differently. I clearly use similar parts of my brain for both. Also, the perspectives gained in one arena can prove helpful in the other, like how we learn from our failures to anticipate the cyclic highs and lows of life and how, in my mother's words, each loss can be an opportunity. Finally, both families and labs are living communities that are constantly changing, evolving, and requiring nimble responses and adaptation to maintain equilibrium.

The two worlds complement each other, like taking refuge in the lab when the children are overwhelmingly noisy or demanding. I was often asked, "How do you deal with three boisterous sons?" My response was always, "It's quite easy. I go to work." Conversely, coming home to loving souls after a paper has been rejected or a grant application denied can be comforting. The satisfaction gained by caring for minor bruises or resolving small conflicts provides respite from the pressures and complexities of scientific life. Additionally, an insular domestic life contrasts with the global nature of our professions. The worldly distractions of a scientific career not only preclude compul-

---

15 Faye Crosby, *Juggling: The Unexpected Advantages of Balancing Career and Home for Women and Their Families* (The Free Press, 1991).

sively controlling and inhibiting a child's development but indeed foster their autonomy.

If only I'd known then what I know now, I would have felt much less guilty about leaving the children with caretakers so that I could go to work. I am reminded of the first time I left one-year-old David to go to a conference at Cold Spring Harbor Laboratory on Long Island, New York. I was a graduate student in California at the time and met my mom in NYC, where she could stay and take care of toddler David at the home of cousins in Queens. But when I returned from Cold Spring Harbor, relieved my presentation at the conference went well and excited to see my baby, he took one look at me and toddled away, pretending he didn't know me or, worse yet, was afraid of me. Big, BIG sigh! The hurt, the guilt, and the fear of negative repercussions were excruciating. If only I had realized then that David was simply learning to express anger without hysteria and practicing separation from me, I would have spared myself a lot of heartache.

In 2002, I was given the Alice C. Evans Award by the American Society for Microbiology (ASM) for my work mentoring young scientists, specifically women. I presented the award talk, "Molecular Microbiology, Motherhood, and Mentoring," at the ASM annual meeting in Salt Lake City, Utah. The Committee on the Status of Women in Microbiology had invited me there to write up my views and experiences regarding the interplay between professional and domestic life, which I did in an article in ASM's magazine *ASM News* titled "Microbiological Moms, Their Sisters and Brothers—the Give and Take."[16] In that article, I addressed the sacrifices and rewards of mothering (and fathering) while mentoring. I discussed the early hurdles, qualities needed to pull both off, and rewards that can be reaped from the effort. I also indicated that "having it all" is a misconception. The sacrifices are several. Time and energy are limited commodities. Starting out in science requires long and sometimes unpredictable

---

16 Marlene Belfort, M, "Microbiological Moms, Their Sisters and Brothers: The Give and Take," *ASM News* 69, no. 11 (November 2003): 553–557.

work hours, needing to be in the lab at midnight to harvest cells at a specific growth phase or to take measurements at fixed times. Most leisure activities end up falling by the wayside.

The time crunch is no joke: I remember having to wait for a snow day before I could find the time to cut my toenails. Pregnancy and breastfeeding can leave you not only exhausted and depleted but deprived of any time to relax. I spent nine years between the ages of twenty-five and thirty-eight either pregnant or nursing—subject to the rigors of "mommydom," if you will. During this time, there were, of course, the physical pressures on my body. But there were also financial burdens, with the relatively pitiful salaries of graduate students, post-docs, and assistant professors restricting childcare options and other lifestyle choices. Then there is the two-body problem affecting couples like me and Georges and exacerbated by the relative paucity of scientific and faculty positions in nonurban locations. It's not like doctor's offices or law firms, which are sprinkled across the landscape. Add this all up and it makes for a lot of sacrifice, no doubt about that, even in areas I haven't mentioned yet, like pursuing hobbies, attending cultural events, and embracing friendships. So, what makes it all worthwhile? Well, if exploration is in your blood, the thrill of discovery can be as riveting as falling in love and as joyful as giving birth.

Although the situation for female scientists is improving, and the 5 percent has grown to about 25 percent, in some ways, I consider myself fortunate to have been of that earlier era when there were so few of us that we needed to act instinctively rather than always rationally. There were no guidelines to follow, no how-to manuals, no mentoring structures, few role models, and no cost–benefit analyses of our future actions. I recall feeling ambivalent about pursuing a career in science versus having children, and there was no one to turn to for advice. So, I muddled through, behaving like a rabbit, procreating when it felt good rather than when it seemed right. Had I been more rational, I might have acted more prudently, postponing childbearing until I was out of training, older, and more mature but with a body less able to withstand the demands of mommydom. There's no strictly right or wrong time to have children, but I'm pleased with the spontaneous decisions I made.

While the lack of support systems in science may have had some unlikely upsides, particularly in how it forced us to extract what we could from our training and do science extemporaneously, it was also a struggle. The courageous fight of Nancy Hopkins together with other talented female faculty to level the playing field for women in science is beautifully documented in the book *The Exceptions*.[17] We owe these women a debt of gratitude for raising awareness of the need for support of women in science. The community is now better able to assist young women by creating institutional policies that are helpful and just, like equitable salaries and lab space, lactation rooms, and parental leave. Support groups are also immensely useful and go a long way toward helping women break through the glass ceiling and smash down the mommy wall. I am a big proponent of all this, and to raise awareness of the predicament women face in science, I give talks on the topic in many different venues, including scientific conferences, research institutions, and universities, even those in such female-*un*friendly environments as Saudi Arabia in the pre–Prince Mohammed bin Salman days and before the opening of Saudi society to women.

Another subject of the *ASM News* article I wrote is the personal attributes necessary for women in STEM to overcome specific biological and societal challenges. What qualities do we need to surmount the difficulties imposed by menstrual cycles, pregnancy, breastfeeding, menopause, and gender-based discrimination, real or perceived? First, in the words of famous biochemist Dr. Arnold Beckman, "There is no satisfactory substitute for excellence."[18] Commitment, drive, and passion are key, as are stamina, patience, decision-making ability, and, once again, *resilience*. Being able to bounce back from rejected

---

17 Kate Zernike, *The Exceptions: Nancy Hopkins and the Fight for Women in Science* (Scribner, 2023).

18 Arnold O Beckman, "7 Rules for Success," The Arnold & Mabel Beckman Foundation, accessed November 21, 2024, https://www.beckman-foundation.org/about-foundation/7-rules-success/.

manuscripts, unfunded grant applications, adverse promotion decisions, and domestic perils like sick children and leaky roofs is vital to moving on. Curiosity and a thirst for discovery are also essential. And then, there is attitude. It is important to be satisfied with "good enough" rather than fixating on every pitfall or letting the need for perfection get in the way of excellence. "Satisficing" (satisfying + sufficing) is an apt term I read recently in a book by Leidy Klotz titled *Subtract*.[19] Yes, satisficing is imperative. Learning to feel okay with compromise and sacrifice is also valuable. And finally, feeling comfortable with nonconformity is very advantageous for women in STEM given how often we need to break with accepted social norms, like, in my day, Mommy not being there to welcome her children home from school, in the same way we defy dogma when presenting a scientific breakthrough to the world. In the wonderful book *Door in the Dream: Conversations with Eminent Women in Science*, Elga Wasserman interviews twenty-five female members of the National Academy of Sciences who have little in common other than the fact they are at peace with their individuality and nonuniform and often interrupted paths to success.[20]

A woman's surroundings and circumstances can make such a huge difference in her life, everything from good fortune to supportive mentoring to exemplary role models, like industrious mothers, smart teachers, talented research colleagues, and successful friends. As mentioned earlier, one aspect of my education that I found very helpful was attending an all-girls school through high school. I had many different female teachers to act as role models, and, again, there was never any relationship in my mind between gender and performance given both the successful students and those who struggled were girls. There is indeed a growing body of literature that indicates girls educated in single-sex environments outperform those in coed environments in science and math. Also, because some girls at school

---

19   Leidy Klotz, *Subtract: The Untapped Science of Less* (Flatiron Books, 2021).
20   Elga Wasserman, *Door in the Dream: Conversations with Eminent Women in Science* (Joseph Henry Press, 2000).

were kind and others were mean, I never associated specific character traits with gender. This meant that as an adult, when I was treated poorly in a professional setting, I tended *not* to view the situation through the lens of gender-based discrimination. That imparted in me a degree of resilience. In short, despite my rocky road to success, I never felt undermined by being a woman.

When it comes to juggling an intense career with a demanding domestic life, help and support are the sine qua non. Family, friends, nannies, housekeepers, childcare centers, community members, and, very importantly, employers can all help lighten the load. I have taken advantage of all these support systems and in the process handed over much of my paycheck for childcare, especially in the early years. But no one factor has been more critical to our success as a family or my scientific accomplishments than my husband Georges's support. He has helped me tremendously on both the domestic and professional fronts, taking care of the children, coaching them, and helping with their homework while also teaching me the physical principles of science in the early days and collaborating in our scientific journey in later years. He is also my cheerleader, nurturing the conviction that I'm able to reach high. Georges also claims our domestic and scientific partnerships have sustained *him* in both his work and home arenas, with me acting as his trusted collaborator and advisor. Most recently, he has been working on using engineering principles to purify mRNA for vaccine development, with me serving as his pro bono advisor. Georges would have no clue about RNA if it weren't for me. And, although it's not always smooth sailing and disagreements sometimes arise, we have always "ridden the winds and broken the waves," as the Chinese idiom goes.

The fulfillment I gain from my roles as a loving mom, nurturing mentor, supportive wife, and successful scientist serve to stabilize my wobbly core, as a child of immigrants who lost her dad to suicide at a young age and always carried that hurt with her. Or maybe a better way to describe it is that the sine waves of life—childhood tragedy, academic triumph, successful marriage, years of pregnancy and nursing, relentless work, tough finances, illness, laughter, and love—have become intertwined to provide the bedrock on which I live and walk into the sunset.

PART THREE

RESILIENCE IN SICKNESS AND IN HEALTH

> "You may not control all the events that happen to you, but you can decide not to be reduced by them."
>
> —MAYA ANGELOU, *LETTER TO MY DAUGHTER*

Some imagine success to involve a steady rise or exponential leap to the top. In both cases, one starts small then moves linearly or logarithmically to the top. For some, that may be true. Lucky them, I suppose. But most of us encounter lots of pitfalls we have to overcome along the way. In her book *The Light We Carry*, Michelle Obama writes, "My power has always hinged on my ability to keep myself out of the ditch," suggesting she *avoided* the pitfalls.[21] In my experience, however, success was much more about falling *into* deep ditches, pulling myself out, and striving to get back on track. For me, success has been all about persistence and resilience.

Resilience, defined as the capacity to recover from difficulties, has a number of components. But most important, I believe, is finding support and working hard and creatively. Overcoming my father's suicide at age thirteen and accepting my inner immigrant as the child of German Jewish refugees involved all that. I found valuable friendships and committed myself to my studies and my dream of becoming a scientist. Climbing up from the depths of grief after my father killed himself was my crash course in resilience training. I strove to excel at school and worked resourcefully to lift myself out of the shame and pain I felt. I also formed close friendships, many of which persist to this day, although we scattered from South Africa and now live throughout the world, in Britain, Israel, Australia, and the US.

The resilience "work" I do today, with the support of my psychiatrist, is to come to terms with residual, unresolved grief. I also strive to create opportunity from loss, as my mom taught me. Of course, this is just a different version of the commonly used phrase, "When life gives you lemons, make lemonade," which we all know is easier said than done. In my case, I've had to struggle for years against my

---

21 Michelle Obama, *The Light we Carry: Overcoming in Uncertain Times* (Crown Press, 2024) 286.

imposter syndrome, both in South Africa and the US, which has its roots in my identity as a child of immigrants and feeling less than. But eventually, I learned to *value* that which made me different, my foreignness, and I did it by surrounding myself with family and friends who appreciate me. That acceptance of my otherness allowed me to explore the fringes, where often the most interesting aspects of life happen and certainly the most creative science lives. In the words of Kurt Vonnegut, "I want to stay as close to the edge as I can without going over. Out on the edge you see all kinds of things you can't see from the center."[22] For me, *that's* the lemonade.

In graduate school, my early trepidation, sense of isolation, and fear of failure drove me to work around the clock, but I was able to harness the support of not only Georges but also Tony Mucci, Georges's former roommate and a graduate student in mathematics. As I clung to those relationships, I was able to ease myself away from the mainstream of science and do original research that earned me admiration. Georges's role in all of this was huge. It was he who tutored me in *all* my areas of weakness, including three semesters' worth of grueling physical chemistry; he who held my hand metaphorically as I took courageous excursions in the lab; and he who encouraged me and loved me all the way. As a result, I graduated with my PhD in four years, having had baby David a year and a half into the program.

Then, there were those two unpleasant work experiences at Wadsworth. I managed to escape both to better situations by, once again, associating with people who cared about and supported me, focusing on my family and my research, and maintaining an impressive track record that propelled me to situations in which I could flourish.

My story took a sharp turn, however, when I was thrust into the mental health crisis you will read about in Chapter Twelve. My resilience was tested in ways I had not expected. But ultimately, to borrow Maya Angelou's evocative turn of phrase, I refused to be "reduced" by these setbacks.

---

22 Kurt Vonnegut, *Player Piano* (Dell, 1952; repr., Random House, 2009), 84.

CHAPTER ELEVEN

RESILIENCE FOR SCIENTISTS

I now teach a course called "Resilience Training for Scientists" to incoming graduate students. It's patterned on a course designed by Dr. Sharon Milgram, director of the Office of Intramural Training and Education at the NIH, and her team. Sharon's course, now offered worldwide, was started near the beginning of the COVID-19 pandemic in 2020 and intended to help NIH trainees overcome obstacles and mental health problems associated with isolation.[23] My course involves webinar presentations and group discussions and deals with the hurdles students need to overcome in their scientific careers, like managing imposter syndrome, developing feedback resilience to scientific criticism and rejection, and maximizing mentoring relationships.

Amid the growing mental health difficulties among our students, we discuss struggles as part of the human condition and shame as a barrier to well-being. But for graduate students, life can be particularly tough because they're no longer being spoon-fed their learning as they

---

23 Becoming a Resilient Scientist (BRS) series, National Institutes of Health, accessed November 21, 2024, https://www.training.nih.gov/wellbeing/join-webinars-and-lectures/brs/.

were as undergraduates; they can't just regurgitate what's been presented to them for an automatic A. They need to think independently and be prepared for failure in a way that's simply foreign to them. For example, having their first abstract heavily critiqued by their thesis advisor and then making all the appropriate revisions only to see their submission rejected is a novel slap in the face. Then there is the arduous journey with those manuscripts that includes multiple rounds of modifications and new experiments before acceptance. Not to mention grants that don't score well enough to be funded. Or how about being scooped in the literature on the very thing they've spent months and sometimes years doing, leaving them with no choice but to scrap much of their precious work and reconfigure what remains? And through all of this, their cognitive distortions loom large. These need to be silenced. Out with, "I am not up to this," and "My writing sucks," and in with, "This is a very competitive system, and I'll get it the next time around!"

So, in addition to all the bad stuff going on in our world, like climate change, toxic politics, and brutal wars, students need to deal with failure. In my class, they learn to make connections with one another in a supportive space and develop their relationships as a community. We talk about wellness practices, like journaling, exercise, hobbies, meditation, and therapy. We also discuss the value of rest and good eating habits. Much of the conversation revolves around their science: how difficult and demanding it is, how failure prone the lab work; the long hours in the lab; the difficulties getting some experiments to work; and the signals they get from their mentors as well as the competition among different cohorts of students. It's a tough life, but it's satisfying to see how these young people build trust in each other and confidence in themselves.

In one of her webinars, Sharon discusses imposter fears and how common they are across professions. She mentions former First Lady Michelle Obama, Starbucks CEO Howard Schultz, actor Tom Hanks, Supreme Court Justice Sonia Sotomayor, and performer Lady Gaga have all experienced imposter syndrome. Then, Sharon interviews

Dr. Francis Collins, the former director of the NIH and scientific rock star I mentioned earlier. Francis describes how he felt after he received his PhD in quantum physics, his MD degree, and did his residency in internal medicine then took a post-doctoral position to learn laboratory-based molecular biology. He was poorly mentored, totally clueless about laboratory science, and felt like a failure when none of his experiments worked. He describes frequent visits to the men's room to cry. (I could certainly relate!) Then, he leaned on a supportive fellow post-doc for help and worked his butt off to propel himself to the highest position in biomedical science in the US and perhaps the world. My students benefit from the course content, guided by Sharon's webinars, my discussion groups, and their mutual support, while I derive great satisfaction from leaning on my bumpy past to pay it forward.

Understanding my own difficulties has allowed me to help my students appreciate theirs and build their strengths around those struggles. As a student, I was forced to build resilience and navigate challenges from the get-go. From entering college without being able to take the necessary chemistry and physics prerequisites, to playing catch-up by being tutored by Georges, to being told at UCT that women are for maternity not chemistry, to proving I could do both, required all the grit I could muster. I also had that rocky post-doc experience at the Hebrew University in Jerusalem. Then, as a fledging independent scientist at Wadsworth Center, the many setbacks, although painful, made me recognize the disapproval I received from resentful bosses was mostly about them rather than me. I fought back by doing the best science I knew how.

It has been said I tend to follow unconventional paths and go against the grain in my work, and perhaps in life, responding to contrarian impulses and striking out in unusual directions. That, too, is the lemonade. I welcome the impression of me as somewhat eccentric. First, because I think it's one of my secrets to success, one of the ingredients to the original thought that is so important to making a mark in science. But also, if it's true what people say about my rebellious thinking, where did that come from? As a child, I longed to fit in with the pack, the opposite of rebelliousness. But maybe that's just it. Maybe I learned at some point to embrace my inner immigrant as an adaptation that promotes accomplishment. Again, the lemonade.

Said differently, rather than undermining me, maybe existing on the fringe powered my creativity.

CHAPTER TWELVE

DEPRESSION IS A DIFFERENT STORY

As a child and young adult, I was unusually healthy. I never suffered more than the flu or a common cold. Even into my forties, my only malady was a melanoma on my arm, which was surgically removed. That was scary, but nothing came close to the terror and agony of late-onset depression. Considering my childhood ordeals and professional traumas, it's remarkable the first time I felt a need to seek therapy was at age forty-six, in the early 1990s. The nest was emptying, with both David and Gabi away at college, and only Yona was still at home. It's perhaps no coincidence that my age then was the same as my father when he killed himself: forty-six.

After shopping around for therapists, I settled on Dr. Gregory Lavigne, a well-trained, smart, and personable psychiatrist. He seemed grounded enough to hold my angst with the right mix of insight, kindness, smarts, and what I would describe as a combination of self-respect and respectfulness. He diagnosed me with dysthymia, a mild form of depression, for which he saw no need for medication. He did, however, recommend psychotherapy to work through my repressed feelings as the child of a suicide victim. Admittedly, I considered therapy unscientific and was therefore skeptical but thought I'd give it a shot. Later, I changed my tune and began to respect therapy in a big way. In fact, I became fascinated by the parallels between the psychoanalytic process and scientific discovery—sifting through feelings versus data and being uncertain of one's findings until the evidence converges on a point, a psychological breakthrough or a scientific fact. But it took me some time before I began to appreciate the parallels between Dr. Lavigne's discipline and my own. I wrote about my experiences with therapy previously in an opinion piece in the *New York Times*.[24]

At first, we spent a great deal of time talking about my birth family, my supportive mom, my loving Oma, Bessie the maid, my slightly problematic brother, and my self-absorbed father, who left us all by driving his car into the Cape Town docks. We also spoke about the tight-knit and loving family that Georges and I have created. Probing the eight months between my dad's disappearance and his discovery felt like a movie in slow motion—we analyzed this interminable and agonizing period in infinitesimal detail, with me responding again and again to the repeated question, "How did that make you feel?" I'd literally never thought about it in those terms, which says something in itself, so it took me a while to answer. But nothing I said seemed too trivial or too outrageous to Dr. Lavigne. After a few years, we stopped therapy, as my dysthymia was well under control. I was happy with how the whole psychotherapy experience had gone, and I felt like it had been instrumental in my recovery.

But then seven years later, at age fifty-three, I began to feel *severely* depressed for the first time ever, and I returned to Dr. Lavigne, who recommended medication. Drugs? What was he thinking? Remember, I delivered three children without medication.

But then, I became desperate and tried all sorts of antidepressants and at outrageously high doses. I started out on Zoloft to manage the

---

[24] Marlene Belfort, "Emotional Abyss; Physical Cause?," *New York Times*, October 30, 2007, https://www.nytimes.com/2007/10/30/health/views/30case.html.

depression, Xanax to control my anxiety, and Ambien to get me to sleep. Then, I went from Zoloft to Paxil and then to Effexor. But my mood remained bleak as I was gripped by discomfort from the side effects of medication: dry mouth, indigestion, a tremor, and brain fog. Lithium was next, but I felt pickled, like acid was refluxing from my stomach and diffusing into all my organs, limbs, and brain. Then Pepcid to counter the reflux, but nothing seemed to help.

In the lab, I was working on an NIH grant renewal application, but I felt like a complete fraud. As the director of the Division of Genetic Disorders, I hid in my administrative office, where I felt "protected" by a receptionist. Convinced I was an imposter and that my deception would soon be revealed, I was unable to eat or sleep. I lost twenty pounds. Then an email from a scientific colleague, Tom Cech, arrived. I was startled to hear from Tom, a friend and Nobel laureate whom I respect greatly. This email, in which Tom asked about my contribution to the intron discovery, sent me over the edge. Not knowing that he was nominating me for the National Academy of Sciences and was doing a simple fact-check, I became psychotic, totally disconnected from reality, imagining the grant I submitted was bogus and convinced I had been faking it throughout my career. I recently found an undated note (but I can tell it's from around this time) that I had handwritten to Georges and our three sons about how badly I had messed up, how my dishonesty was a tragedy for us all, and how it was going to be my fault when all our lives were ruined when all I really wanted was to be the best mom and wife. Seeing the note brought me right back to that dark time, when an innocent email about a work matter could trigger that kind of meltdown in me. But that *is* how I was feeling back then: hollow, guilty, confused, and psychotic.

Even when I learned the real reason Tom asked about the intron discovery, it only made matters worse, if you can believe it. With the news of my successful Academy nomination, my psychic pain became unbearable. I agonized over being a scientific fake, and Dr. Lavigne's recommendation was that I be admitted to a psychiatric hospital, Four Winds in Saratoga Springs, New York. Georges and Yona, who was home from college at the time, drove me to Saratoga one afternoon in November 1998, as the days were getting colder and shorter. I sat in the car, trembling, ruminating over my father's suicide, and recalling the story of his brother Walter. Onkel Walter (who had been married to my dear Tante Alice) apparently went through some mental health challenge in his thirties and had to be admitted to a psychiatric hospital, Valkenberg, in Cape Town. He spent the rest of his life there. Was I going to be kept at Four Winds for the rest of my days? Was I going mad like Onkel Walter? I was drenched in fear and pained to the core.

When we finally got to Four Winds, I resisted admission, literally kicking and screaming for hours on end, but was eventually pacified by the physicians and admissions staff. To this day, it's hard for me to imagine behaving that way, but it was like I was a different person. After I signed the admission papers, the staff did a body search, presumably for weapons I might use to harm myself or others. They also searched my handbag and confiscated my nail scissors and the tweezers I used to pluck my eyebrows. "Sorry, no sharps allowed!" It felt like in addition to my belongings, my freedom was being confiscated. I didn't care about possessions, but autonomy was important to me, even in the extreme depths of my despair.

After the admissions staff calmed me down, they handed Georges, Yona, and me each a Patient and Family Handbook outlining the treatment philosophy "to facilitate a positive self-esteem and healthy identity," daily patient routines, and visiting guidelines for family and friends. Then, they turned to Georges and Yona, asked if they had any questions, and told them it was time to say goodbye. There were heart-wrenching hugs and tears, and then, they walked out into the night as I was escorted to my ward.

The staff on the ward settled me in and provided more handouts. It felt like the first day of classes, except instead of saying SYLLABUS, the initial handout said ADULT SERVICE INPATIENT PROGRAM SCHEDULE. It listed many skills trainings: increasing personal effectiveness, coping with depression, improving stress tolerance, managing emotions, and so on, and every training had its own set of handouts. There were also offerings in meditation and art therapy and daily psychotherapy sessions, both individual and group, and more handouts that had been photocopied to the point of blurriness. *I'm a good student, I can do this*, I thought. The staff took excellent care of me, and at times, I felt "held," like a baby, and that made me feel good, recalling my mother's care. But the depression persisted. I was very diligent, busy all day taking advantage of the various offerings and meeting frequently with my psychiatric team, but nothing came close to snapping me out of my misery.

Then, one day, the chief of Inpatient Psychiatry, Dr. Michael Priest, came by to tell me I was a candidate for the dreaded shock therapy, also called "electroconvulsive therapy," or ECT. For those who have not seen *One Flew Over the Cuckoo's Nest* with Jack Nicholson or read the Ken Kesey novel on which it's based, you should know that ECT is not fun. The procedure involves full anesthesia and electric shocks to the brain, leaving the patient feeling weak and with severe, albeit mostly temporary, short-term memory loss. But the ECT *did* help. My depression lifted, and I was discharged thirteen days after being admitted, with instructions to complete my shock treatments as an outpatient.

In the months that followed, I suffered three relapses of major depression; none was as severe as the first, but only high doses of antidepressants and talk therapy kept me from rehospitalization. The relapses had me enveloped in darkness, without energy and unable to function at home or work. When the children visited, I was incapable of setting the table, let alone cooking the customary multicourse meal. The only productive act I could manage was doing laundry. Dr. Lavigne kept asking if I was suicidal. The answer was a resounding NO; I had no suicidal ideation whatsoever. How could I possibly inflict the pain that was wrought on me on Georges and our children? I might have felt like a scientific fraud, but as I recovered, the mom part of me triumphed. When I asked Yona many years later how he felt during that period, he spoke of his trauma and fear about what was going to happen to me "and all of us." Then he said, "Ma, when I visited you at Four Winds after an ECT treatment, you were dazed but happy to see me. When I kissed you on your forehead, it was still greasy with the gel they used to place the electrodes." Later, he added, "Mom, I tend now to focus on the things I *can* control. I wonder if that's what got me through that period or if this is what Four Winds taught me." My fear was that my illness was crushing my children; little did I know I was helping build *their* resilience.

After the worst of it was over, Dr. Lavigne remained puzzled by the sudden onset of my first major depressive episode at age fifty-three. Right after I was hospitalized at Four Winds, he asked if my PCP (primary care physician) had ordered any blood tests. PCP? I didn't know what the acronym stood for. I had been so healthy up to this point that I had no PCP. But after my second relapse, Dr. Lavigne insisted I find one and have blood work done. Sure enough, my serum calcium and parathyroid hormone (PTH) levels were elevated, indicative of an endocrine condition called "hyperparathyroidism." He pointed out a potential link to depression. Indeed, medical students are taught the mnemonic "painful bones, renal stones, and *psychic moans*" to recall symptoms of hypercalcemia and hyperparathyroidism.

I had surgery to control the parathyroid problem and then monitoring of both my blood chemistry and moods, but neither improved. During that operation, the surgeon removed three and a half of my four parathyroid glands, but my calcium levels and PTH levels remained stubbornly high and my mood stubbornly low for months on end. After additional radioactive scans, it was discovered I had an unusual, fifth, ectopic gland. So, after my third relapse into major depression, I had to get a second surgery, two years after the first. Sure enough, the calcium and PTH levels returned to normal, as did my moods. Georges and I gathered data and plotted graphs from more than ten years of recorded calcium and PTH levels, medications, and depression severity. The correlation between depression and hyperparathyroidism, as monitored by elevated calcium and PTH levels, was so impressive I wrote the abovementioned essay for the *New York Times* in 2007 entitled "Emotional Abyss; Physical Cause?"[25] In that

---

25   Belfort, "Emotional Abyss; Physical Cause?"

article, I recounted the same story I've shared here of my protracted illness. I wondered if doctors might routinely explore a physical basis for sudden, late-onset depression and also if my father may have suffered from hyperparathyroidism. The essay ends with these prophetic words, "Of course, I may not be permanently cured of depression. My time in the abyss opened a place whose door will always remain ajar."

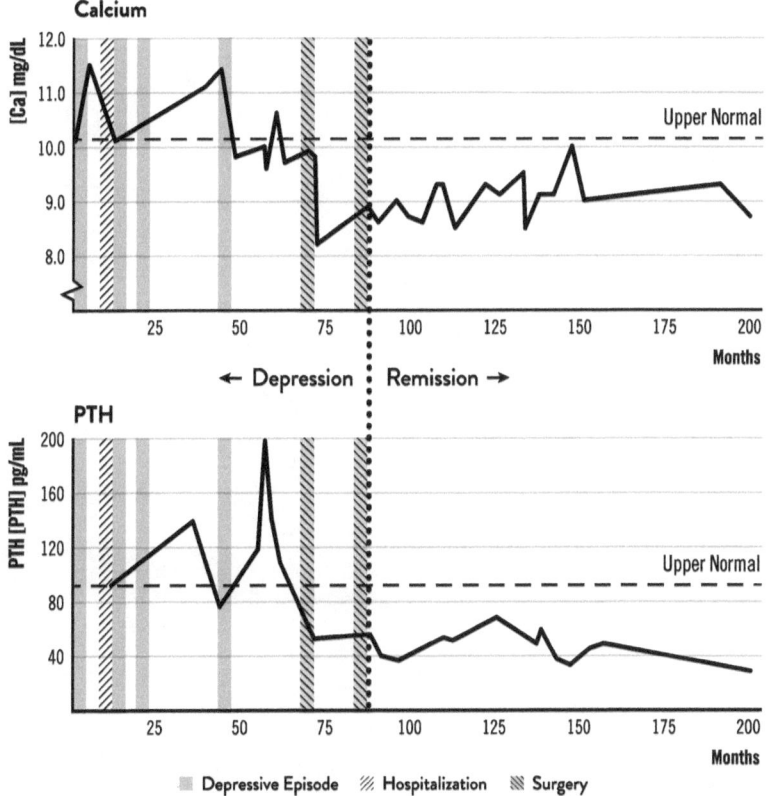

DEPRESSION AND HYPERPARATHYROIDISM: There's an amazing coincidence of elevated calcium **(top)** and parathyroid hormone levels **(PTH, bottom)** with depressive episodes **(grey bars, left of dotted line)**. Hospitalization was at Four Winds psychiatric hospital in Saratoga Springs, New York. The spike in PTH at about fifty months correlated with lithium administration, designed to treat the depression. Surgeries reflect removal of parathyroid glands, after which there was prolonged remission from depression **(right of dotted line)**.

CHAPTER THIRTEEN

THE DOOR TO DEPRESSION REMAINS AJAR

All was well for thirteen years. Complete remission for thirteen years! Then, a tick bite on Cape Cod, probably from when Georges and I were picking veggies on a farm with our grandchildren, landed me in the hospital for five days with a parasitic illness called "babesiosis." What alerted Georges to a problem was that, unusually, I slept the entire drive back to Albany from the Cape. Then, in the middle of the night, I fell when going to the bathroom, retching. He picked me up off the floor in our bedroom, cleaned me up, and rushed me to the hospital. I had raging fevers, fainting spells, chills, and was in atrial fibrillation when admitted. It took two days for the babesiosis diagnosis, from which point I was treated with an antibiotic combination and the symptoms rapidly subsided. My temperature dropped, and my heart reverted to normal sinus rhythm (although later, they implanted a pacemaker, just to be safe). But not long after my hospitalization for babesiosis, the door that was ajar burst open to a full-blown major depressive episode.

We went through the same drill as before. I first saw Dr. Lavigne for psychotherapy and to adjust my meds. Then, at my wit's end when nothing helped lift the depression, I consulted a psychopharmacologist, a distant relative in New York. Together, the two physicians put me through a long list of antidepressants and antipsychotics, and I tried an alphabet-soup of drugs I'd not used before, some in series, others in combination: Abilify, Cymbalta, Klonopin, Remeron, Rexulti, Seroquel, Synthroid, Wellbutrin. Again, I felt dehydrated, numb, fogged up, unable to sleep, thoroughly discouraged, and staring into a dark void. After several months on complex and unhelpful drug regimens and wallowing in hopelessness, Dr. Lavigne once again recommended hospitalization.

So, there I was again, at Four Winds in a drugged-up stupor. This time, I went willingly, and my admission was without incident. Again, I felt well treated by the staff, but again, the depression did not lift, and I became a candidate for ECT. The difference now, however, was that I had a pacemaker and needed to have the shock therapy at a major medical center. We elected to go with Dr. Kerry Bloomingdale at Beth Israel Deaconess Hospital in Boston. This meant three-hour drives each way and overnight stays in the Boston area starting at the end of January 2019, initially several times a week and later less frequently, for a total of sixteen exhausting treatments over almost four months. Imagine what this must have felt like for Georges, enduring the physical burden of the drive and the emotional toll of caring for someone who was seriously depressed. We usually stayed with one of our two Boston-based sons and their family, and we were welcomed with open arms, but what would normally be a joyful experience was plagued by worry and anguish. Although I always felt cradled and loved by them, after each treatment, I was spacey and in no position to interact with anyone. I can only envision how sad and scary this must have been for them.

My sleep was highly disturbed, and I felt depleted and desperate. However, after ECT treatment, I tended to be groggy and sometimes fell into a deep sleep. I therefore welcomed the anesthesia. But when the effects of the shock therapy and anesthetic wore off, I suffered from wakefulness again, spending long nights staring into a dark vacuum despite taking hypnotics, sedatives, and sleep aids of various kinds. The mind plays nasty tricks during those hours of sleeplessness, placing worst-case scenarios front and center and leading to days of exhaustion from battling the demons at night. Sleep deprivation is bothersome at the best of times, even when one is in good health, but during these lengthy depressive periods, it once again robbed me of any respite from the psychological pain.

Georges was my primary caregiver throughout these lengthy depressive episodes, the first spanning about five years starting in 1998, when I was fifty-three, and the second beginning in 2017 and going for two years, when I was in my early seventies. During these periods, our usual dynamic flipped in all sorts of ways. Typically, I was the one who indulged and coddled Georges; now, he was responsible for taking care of *me* and the whole household. He went from living with an equal partner to one who was thoroughly dependent, from traveling around the globe to being stuck at home, from being with a friend to feeling alone. He took on many other tasks as well, like battling our health insurance company to cover my mental health care as well as communicating with my medical providers, coworkers, and friends. And of course, our children. He also kept records of my medical tests and moods and did what he does best: He plotted data. Much as he had previously generated graphs relating my blood chemistry to depression, this time he graphed Hamilton scores, an assessment tool based on a questionnaire used to indicate the depth of depression. The higher the score, the worse the depression. Imagine our disillusionment when for the first five ECT treatments, the Hamilton scores remained stratospheric. So, they upped the current of the electric shock and administered the treatment to both hemispheres of my brain rather than just one. Bilateral ECT totally shot my short-term memory and made me feel like a zombie, but miraculously, my mood started to improve, and the Hamilton score eventually dropped to zero.

Meanwhile, Georges's form of journaling to maintain his sanity was keeping a log of my ECT treatments, my moods, and his communication with my physicians and our children. The following is just one of his many entries. This one is from after my ninth ECT treatment on February 22, 2019, at a point when I was well on the road to recovery:

> **FRIDAY 2/22/19 ECT #9 8:20-10:00 A.M.**
>
> Today, Friday, has been a tough day for Mom, although her Hamilton scores are improved. This was by far the most intense effect of the ECT on her. She was tired all day—did not speak much. We took a walk near Dave and Mandy's, and she wanted to return after fifteen minutes (we usually walk for forty minutes). Bloomingdale told me that it is common for people's subjective perception of their mood to lag behind that of other people or behind scores on instruments like the Hamilton Scale. I took her to lunch in Newton Center and received a parking ticket. She lay next to me most of the afternoon and dozed. Then we watched the BBC and NPR news and she dozed again during the news. She ate supper and proceeded to go to bed early at 8:00 p.m. I just checked, and she was deep asleep.
>
> Saturday, she recovered after a good night's sleep (no meds), and on Sunday, we attended Lincoln's (Gabi's son's) swimming meet—loved it but she felt faint from the heat and humidity inside the pool area—had to sit outside. We watched Man U vs. Liverpool in the evening. Looked after the kids while Mandy and Dave went out for a date (movie and dinner)—they were all wonderful. Marl did not sleep well on Sunday eve. Worried about getting to the hospital on time for Monday's treatment. Bloomingdale pleased today, and mom said she was doing better. Marl prepared and submitted a twelve-page report to NIH for one of her grants. She also has reviewed two manuscripts in detail.

Clearly, I was exhausted from the ECT treatment, but thankfully, I was on the mend and beginning to function and be in control of my life again. Also, between treatments, I was no longer on heavy medication. Georges noticed I was becoming more assertive with him again and would even sometimes express my annoyance. He called this his "Irritation Index," observing that when I was depressed, I tended to be meek and compliant, and taking my feistiness as a good sign.

Hamilton Depression Score

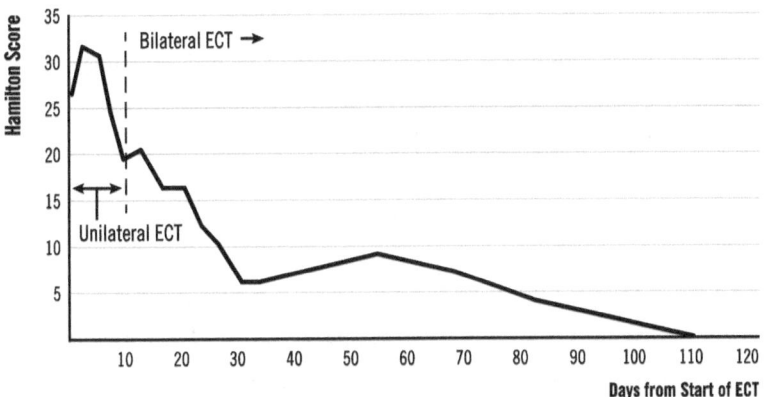

EFFECTIVE TREATMENT OF DEPRESSION WITH ECT, 2019: Hamilton depression scores (0 = not depressed, 35 = extremely depressed) are plotted against time (days). It took a while for those scores to come down.

The Hamilton index was a useful guide to evaluate my recovery. It went to zero toward the sixteenth and last treatment, after four months, and I felt great. Dr. Bloomingdale joked that I had graduated. The same day as my last ECT treatment, Georges took me for a consult with Dr. Maurizio Fava, a world-renowned professor of psychiatry at Massachusetts General Hospital. The visit was arranged by Gabi, a colleague of Dr. Fava's, because he wanted an independent evaluation of my condition. Dr. Fava approved of the two meds I was still taking and advised against walking in woods and touching branches to guard against insect-borne diseases like West Nile virus, lime disease, and babesiosis, which are rampant in the Northeast. He also said to avoid infections by being well vaccinated (pneumonia and shingles were two examples he gave). He explained that the body releases large amounts of inflammatory cytokines (cytokine storms) after infection and these can cause depression in those predisposed, as I obviously am. Dr. Fava also cautioned me to control my blood pressure and cholesterol, as hypertension and high cholesterol are risk factors for depression, and he told me to reduce stress whenever possible. Also, I needed to address any recurring symptoms immediately should they arise. After an hour and a half, he declared me in complete remission. That was almost six years ago. Perhaps most happily, Dr. Fava told us he knows of nothing in the literature to suggest late-onset depression is hereditary and that it seems to result from life's traumas, of which I've certainly had my fair share. That was great news for Dr. Fava's friend Gabi and for us all.

It's scary living so close to the edge, but I feel grateful for my return to a normal life and the sparks of joy that now exist in me again. There's no escaping those two extremely debilitating episodes of depression thirteen years apart, and occasionally, if I'm feeling ill or exhausted or stressed, I worry that the door to depression will fling open yet again. For example, recently, three and a half years into the pandemic, I contracted COVID-19 for the first time. I recovered quickly but then relapsed a week later. Would a release of cytokines send me back into depression? So far, so good, but it's like having survived a flood, when each drizzle signals an impending rainstorm, or more relevant to my current reality at age seventy-nine, when each new freckle could become a melanoma. It's hard to put the deep despair entirely in the rearview mirror.

Recently, I discussed my major depression with my brother-in-law, David Bernard, Georges's sister Ethel's husband, a South African–trained physician who now lives in Manhattan. I have consulted with David about various ills over the years, and I told him of Georges's plotting Hamilton scores and how they didn't drop for the first five ECT treatments. Rather than providing a possible explanation, David said, "Marl, that must have been extremely discouraging." I replied that, at the time, discouragement had no place to go; I was already at rock bottom in an abyss so black it could get no darker. He asked me about my moods as a young person, and I couldn't recall any real lows, other than when my dad died. So, I asked my friend Sandra Wyner about my moods in college. Sandra and I were very close, two of the few "science girls." She often lived with us at my home in Oranjezicht. We studied together, we socialized, and we were flatmates in London. She said that she saw me as happy, a little wild, and the last person she'd thought could get depressed. Sandra also commented on how industrious I was and optimistic: I never "saw the dark side," in her words. Apparently, I didn't talk of my father's suicide at all, and we found that remarkable, but then neither did she speak of her mom's alcoholism. Keeping the sadness buried appears to have been our way of coping. I wonder if my industriousness was, or even is, a defense against the dark side? I also wonder what might have happened if I had been taught as a child how to process my grief. Would I have had less of a need to metabolize my sadness as an adult? Might I have been spared these major depressive episodes?

Of course, as a biologist, I remain fascinated and perplexed by the unknowns of my late-onset depression and the two extreme depressive episodes separated by more than a decade with nothing but mild dysthymia between, before, or after. The etiology of the two episodes was different, at least at first blush, but there are possible correlations. It is well known that hypercalcemia can cause changes in central nervous system function that lead to psychosis and depression, but elevated PTH levels also can be accompanied by an increase in inflammatory markers.[26] And, as noted by Dr. Fava, there is a strong relationship between inflammatory cytokines and depression, as discussed further below, which is thought to have provoked the second episode after the babesiosis infection. I also wonder if the joint action of hypercalcemia and a cytokine response in that first major depressive episode potentiated a form of depression that can now be stimulated by inflammation alone.

It is noteworthy that cytokines are important for normal brain function and can therefore influence behaviors and moods as well as acting as mediators of environmental stress.[27] I wonder if the stress

---

[26] Kristin A. Parks et al., "Psychiatric Complications of Primary Hyperparathyroidism and Mild Hypercalcemia," *American Journal of Psychiatry* 174, no. 7 (July 2017): 620–622, https://doi.org/10.1176/appi.ajp.2017.16111226; Shih-Ping Cheng et al., "Association Between Parathyroid Hormone Levels and Inflammatory Markers Among US Adults," *Mediators of Inflammation* 2014, no. 1 (March 2014): 709024, https://doi.org/10.1155/2014/709024.

[27] Jennifer C. Felger and Francis E. Lodrich, "Inflammatory Cytokines in Depression: Neurobiological Mechanisms and Therapeutic Implications," *Neuroscience* 246 (May 2013): 199–229, https://doi.org/10.1016/j.neuroscience.2013.04.060.

of maintaining a funded lab might have been an underlying cause in both bouts of depression. During the first episode back in 1998, I was working on an NIH grant renewal when I became psychotic (the grant scored in the top few percentile and was funded despite my worst fears), whereas in 2017, I was plagued by whether I should renew my two NIH grants or shut down my lab and move toward retirement. The grants had each been continuously funded for more than thirty years, and to renew, I would need to become proficient in bioinformatics for big-data analysis. Although I had successfully pivoted into new disciplines on several previous occasions, like DNA recombination and RNA structure, I asked myself if I was prepared to immerse myself in learning sophisticated computational tools? On the other hand, was I ready to close my lab, lay my scientific baby to rest, and give up my identity as a researcher? I elected the latter, which was an agonizing decision but once made, opened new opportunities.

CHAPTER FOURTEEN

EACH LOSS IS AN OPPORTUNITY

This has been a difficult part of the book to write. In its first iteration, this section was filled with data on PTH and calcium levels, analysis of that data, carefully annotated mood-med charts, and a litany of detailed records kept by Georges about what the doctors said, how I was feeling, and how *he* interpreted how I was feeling. I've now condensed some of that material to two graphs in the previous chapters (the scientist in me can't completely get rid of data) and dumped the rest. But what was I hiding? What do *I* have to say? It's clearly easier for me to interpret data than plumb the soul. Facing one's grief is painful work that takes huge courage. But reacquainting myself with that vulnerable girl who was abandoned by her father, that child who was so insignificant she was not worth hanging around for, has its rewards. Acknowledging this inner ache provides an understanding of powerlessness as a driving force to become stronger and be seen. Maybe I have my father to thank for propelling me to become a forceful scientist and a formidable mom.

But this part of the book has also been hard to write because of those who love me, those who see me as a force and a rock in their lives. I fear they put their painful recollections aside like a bad dream and this exposé will push the awful memories front and center again. I also worry my children fear for themselves and their offspring, that the dreaded predisposition to late-onset depression has been passed along to them and they may transfer it to *their* children. They are now in midlife, beyond the age my father was when he killed himself (whew!) but approaching the life stage at which I succumbed to that first episode of debilitating paranoia and depression. Dr. Fava's opinion that late-onset depression is environmentally induced rather than genetically transmitted is reassuring, particularly because my kids were spared major childhood traumas. Nevertheless, this is a hard cross for them to bear that also reinforces their bonds to me and with each other.

Writing this memoir has been cathartic for me and has me looking at the bright side of these dreadfully painful and lengthy depressions. I've never been great at the recommended "journaling," but documenting my life has been a form of retrospective recording. It highlights for me the inner strength I've mustered to bounce back, the courage it took to think outside the box, and the value of leaning on others. Also, being public about my inner struggles and vulnerabilities has quenched the shame associated with my childhood and with the depressions themselves. I've also learned from the experiences in ways that help me stay balanced and open-minded as I navigate life.

I am reminded, for example, of all I learned during my first pregnancy. Georges and I took Lamaze classes with a certified labor coach and diligently attended every session. Georges would lie beside me with a stopwatch from the lab and issue the command, "Contractions begin!" I also practiced the breathing exercises at home, repeating them several times a day without his prompts because I wanted to have a natural, unmedicated delivery. I succeeded on that front. But my labor was long and excruciating, and nothing could have prepared me for the agony of childbirth. It felt like a door kept banging on my finger, except it was banging in my pelvis and stretching and squeezing all my organs. Lamaze went out the delivery-room window. However, to this day, whenever I'm in mild pain, like when I'm sitting in the dentist's chair, I practice Lamaze breathing. When dealing with situations less painful than childbirth, I find it very helpful in relaxing me and helping me overcome discomfort. Likewise, all the mindfulness and meditation practices, the dialectical behavior therapy, the daily physical exercise, the focus on the subtle sights and sounds and tastes may have made no dent in relieving my depression, but I am grateful for them because they help me live a more relaxed and calm life. All the exercises, physical and psychological, I've learned have built a more resilient me. I refuse to waste the loss of self I experienced during depression and would rather use it to move me forward.

PART FOUR

PARTNERSHIPS IN SCIENCE AND IN LIFE

> *"The fundamental law of human beings is interdependence. A person is a person through other persons."*
>
> —Archbishop Desmond Tutu

Archbishop Desmond Tutu, the South African theologian and human-rights and anti-Apartheid activist, got it all right. In his opposition to racial segregation and white-minority rule, he encouraged collective peaceful protests, which he combined with foreign economic pressure from multiple countries to effect change. He knew he simply could not do it alone.

From an early age, I recognized I needed to join hands with those around me, both literally and figuratively, such as with my teenage school friends to overcome the stigma of my father's suicide and with boyfriends to help repair my battered self-image. Then, I needed Georges's help to not only prepare me for a career in science but also assist me in navigating that career through collaboration, acting as my sounding board, and guiding me through difficult professional decisions. He also helped piece me together when I was broken. And that is to say nothing of his co-parenting our children, which was critical to freeing me to do my work and vital to raising whole people.

Scientific collaborations took many different forms throughout my career, both within my laboratory and with scientists down the hallway, across town, around the country, and throughout the world. Often, the magic would happen when our work intersected the bounds of our different scientific disciplines. A point made earlier was that living close to the fringe makes the lemonade happen. These collaborative relationships were not free of their tensions, but there's no question I made it to where I am today by embracing giants, playing with them in the sandbox of science, and standing on their shoulders.

Then, there are the women in my life who nurtured me and helped me grow: my mom, Oma, Bessie, the girls at Good Hope, and the women's groups I've joined and formed. They have all guided and sustained me, helped me look inside myself—and like what I found—and allowed me in turn to nourish other women and build diverse communities. I am who I am through their insights, honesty, trust, love, and support.

CHAPTER FIFTEEN

SCIENTIFIC COLLABORATIONS ARE WONDERFUL BUT FRAUGHT

Laughter and foreign accents would fill the air at Georges's and my joint Belfort-backyard lab parties, of which there were many over the years at Playfields, our home. Typically, among the students, post-docs, and faculty, only a handful were US born, with the rest from Africa, Asia, Europe, and the Middle East. That's the texture of many US and European labs these days: a potpourri of nationalities that makes the science happen. Foreigners transform our labs into exciting international hubs, elevating our science and exposing American trainees and technicians to other cultures, making them citizens of the world without ever leaving our shores. At the same time, the trainees from the two Belfort labs would interact not only on the volleyball court but across the biology–engineering divide, helping forge a much-valued interlaboratory and interdisciplinary collaboration.

Helping foreign trainees settle in was a fun challenge. We provided a home away from home until they found a place to live, fed them alongside our family, and gave them maps to find their way in the days before smartphones. We have lifelong relationships with some of these trainees, who are now senior scientists in their home countries, providing us friendships from Beijing to Bologna and Tel Aviv to Tokyo. They share their triumphs long distance, including weddings, promotions, and important papers published, and also life's setbacks, like illnesses in the family, divorces, and the loss of loved ones. Some still visit on occasion, when they have a meeting in the US, and we reciprocate as opportunities arise on our travels abroad. For example, Georges and I on our way to a recent conference in Prague visited nearby Vienna to meet Renée Schroeder and Michael Kremsner, who trained in our respective labs decades ago. We feel enriched by these former students and post-docs, who remain part of the fabric of our lives.

WITH FORMER POST-DOC IN AUSTRIA, 2024: Visiting Renée Schroeder, former post-doc **(left)**, in the Alps, with friend Michael Sherer and Georges **(right)**.

In examining my publication record, I realized almost half the papers have authors from outside my laboratory. Most of those coauthors are from regional labs, with about a quarter from around the country and some 10 percent being international. Collaborations are enticing and scary, exhilarating and fraught; they undoubtedly add to the strength of our science while also requiring huge trust and strict guidelines. They are cornerstones of modern research, with an increasingly large number of authors appearing on scientific papers.

Much has been written about scientific collaboration. In my own field of bacterial genetics, François Jacob, who won the 1965 Nobel Prize in Physiology or Medicine with his colleague Jacques Monod, wrote of their collaboration, "It's more enjoyable to work in pairs than alone. For with two minds working on a problem, ideas fly thicker and faster. They are bounced from partner to partner. They are grafted onto each other like branches on a tree. And in the process, illusions are sooner nipped in the bud."[28]

The obvious rewards of collaboration are enormous. They allow for an exchange of ideas and a combining of disciplines that are impossible to achieve working alone. Creativity as a group process has me thinking about my son Yona, who introduced me to the concept of "brainstorming" when he was a graduate student in product design at Stanford in the late 1990s. The students from many different backgrounds, like engineering, art, and medicine, were trained to spontaneously volunteer solutions to a design problem in a freethinking format until, oftentimes, a visionary product would emerge. We adopted brainstorms at our lab meetings, with great success. I would often do a brainstorm with my trainees when I was stumped by a research problem, and we would free associate and come up with ideas that frequently provided a solution or took us in a new direction.

Equally important is the merging of disciplines, where many different specializations are brought to bear on a modern scientific problem. In that sense, collaborations can be like an orchestra, where disci-

---

28 François Jacob, *Of Flies, Mice and Men*, trans. Giselle Weiss (Harvard University Press, 1999).

plines are the equivalent of musical instruments and the lead scientist is the conductor, using her or his talents to merge the disciplines into a symphony of scientific discovery. This all sounds quite beautiful, but scientific collaborations can also be difficult. One most certainly needs to own a new concept before slicing it up and apportioning it among collaborators, a little like knowing how to be alone before one can be fully with someone else.

Collaborations can also be fraught by the need to *share*, as in authorship, credit, reagents, and intellectual property. As a result, tensions, jealousies, and competitiveness can arise, and clear guidelines for collaboration are therefore required. We need to weigh such matters as the sharing of data and reagents, division of labor, coauthorship and order of contributors in published papers, access to unpublished data, and ownership of intellectual property. Volumes have been written on these topics, with input from scientists, businesspeople, and lawyers. My major concern is protecting my trainees, the instruments of collaborative science, so *they* receive the appropriate credit to propel them into their future careers. And although I sometimes have come out of a collaboration feeling battered and bruised, my trainees seem to have emerged not only unscathed but all the stronger for the collective enterprise. I consider myself fortunate in that way.

My own science has benefited massively from collaboration at local, national, and international levels. Together, we took the research to higher levels than I might have achieved on my own. My local colleagues brought all sorts of different backgrounds to these collaborations: the Maleys in protein chemistry, David Shub in phage T4 biology, Joan Curcio in retrotransposons and yeast genetics, Kathleen McDonough in infectious disease, Patrick van Roey in X-ray crystallography, and Georges Belfort in quantitative analysis and transport phenomena. At the national level, Alan Lambowitz, another intron expert, and I have had a fruitful collaboration over decades on the knife's edge of friendship and competitiveness. He has been like a brother in science, offering a mix of support and rivalry. We had fun playing in the intron sandbox together, and as we cultivated our joint science, it soared to new heights. But there existed a creative tension, and I constantly needed to be on the lookout to protect my interests.

An example of a successful international collaboration began after a decade of struggle on a research project involving the structure of an intron RNA complexed with a protein with which it coexists in the cell. We needed to understand how the protein and RNA, both enzymes, interact. It turns out the best way to image the complex was by a technique called "cryo-electron microscopy" (cryo-EM), where the sample is embedded in ice to preserve its natural features. However, ten years of effort with my Wadsworth Center colleague Joachim Frank revealed only the size and shape of the intron complex but no detail—like seeing a person's face with only blobs and depressions as major features. My patience was running thin. Then, almost a decade ago, there was a revolution in cryo-EM technology. At about that time, we started a collaboration with Dr. Hongwei Wang, then an assistant professor at Yale. He soon moved to Tsinghua University in Beijing, China, which had one of the very best cryo-EM facilities in the world. We performed the genetics and biochemistry in Albany to purify the particles that Hongwei then imaged in Beijing. Hongwei and I became friends and trusted colleagues.

Although the distance seemed formidable, we soon learned how to have meetings by Skype (before the days of Zoom and Webex) and send frozen specimens to Beijing. Our PhD students visited back and forth between Beijing and Albany, but still, we saw only vague shapes. I worried the specimens we had painstakingly prepared and carefully transported across oceans were inferior. Then, one day, Hongwei emailed that we needed to Skype immediately; he was able to analyze many more particles, and the resolution of the images was four times better than anything we'd seen before. A few weeks later, the images were almost ten times better! Using the face analogy, at four times, we could see exactly where the eyes, nose, and mouth were in broad outline; at ten times, we could see great detail, the eyes and eyelashes, facial contours, and freckles. In molecular terms, we could view the protein and RNA molecules embracing intimately and even in some parts observe their atoms communicating. We were thrilled.

Hongwei and I then collaborated with a third partner, Dr. Raj Agrawal at Wadsworth. Raj refined the model we published in 2016 in a premier British journal, *Nature Structural and Molecular Biology*.[29] This article—written by three scientists, one Chinese (Hongwei), one Indian (Raj, now a US citizen), and one South African (me, now also a US citizen), along with our international trainees—was accompanied by an editorial highlighting its breakthrough status.[30] It saddens me that such productive collaborations with talented Chinese colleagues are becoming rarer these days because of international tensions, specifically over allegations that the Chinese are committing scientific espionage. After all, science is a common language that transcends national, political, and cultural boundaries. For the good of humankind, we need to share our science across these divides. But we live in a troubled world.

Finally, I need to emphasize that as scientists and pilots of our own life journeys, we must be prepared to leap into uncertainty and take risks. Doing that *while holding hands* promises joint experiences that are more likely to end in success through the merging of talents (in contrast to a more controlled solo flight). When it comes to the science, collaborations can catapult the research. Sure, there are some new risks introduced by working together, but collaboration also mitigates other risks, like falling behind and missing discoveries. Let us not forget that the synergy created by merging talents, resources, and disciplines, sometimes across continents, often propels the scientific enterprise.

---

29 Guosheng Qu et al., "Structure of a Group II Intron in Complex with Its Reverse Transcriptase," *Nature Structure and Molecular Biology* 23 (2016): 549-57, https://doi.org/10.1038/nsmb.3220.

30 Joseph A. Piccirilli and Jonathan P. Staley, "Reverse Transcriptases Lend a Hand in Splicing Catalysis," *Nature Structure and Molecular Biology* 23 (2016): 507-509, https://doi.org/10.1038/nsmb.3242.

CHAPTER SIXTEEN

A COUPLE THAT DOES SCIENCE TOGETHER...

There are many examples of spousal partnerships in science. These date back at least to Antoine Lavoisier, who discovered the role of oxygen in combustion, being assisted by fellow chemist and wife Marie-Anne Paulze Lavoisier in the eighteenth century, a couple known also for being members of the French nobility. A century later, in 1903, the French–Polish couple Marie and Pierre Curie won the Nobel Prize in Physics for their discovery of radioactivity. Fast forward another century, and there was my friend Joan Steitz at Yale who published an occasional paper with her Nobel Prize–winning husband, Tom. And there were Georges's friends and colleagues Jay Bailey and Frances Arnold, who were married and both enjoyed faculty positions as chemical engineers at Caltech. Jay was offered a high-profile position at ETH Zurich, a university in Switzerland, but the best they could do for Frances was provide some nebulous position in Polymer Science, so Frances decided to stay at Caltech. Unfortunately, Jay passed away prematurely in Switzerland in the early 2000s, whereas Frances went on to be awarded the Nobel Prize in

Chemistry in 2018 for her work on the directed evolution of enzymes, the first female engineer to be so honored. Fortunately for Caltech, that university made the right decision.

I also know of a type of partnership where husband and wife share the same academic position; each one holds a 50 percent appointment, and together, they earn one full salary. Our friends and former neighbors in Slingerlands Sharon and George Gmelch are cultural anthropologists who shared the same academic position; each one held a 75 percent appointment, and together they earned one and a half full salaries at both Union College and at the University of San Francisco. Of their many books, they have coauthored four, ranging from work in cultural anthropology to wine tourism in the Napa Valley. Kudos to Sharon and George for making job sharing work; I'm not sure it wouldn't make Georges and me crazy.

In contrast, Georges and I have independent positions at different institutions across the Hudson River from each other, he at RPI in Troy, New York, and me at UAlbany. We work together for about 10 percent of our professional lives, separated not just by the river but also by the bounds of molecular biology and chemical engineering. Roughly 10 percent of our papers are coauthored, bringing together the elements of engineering and fundamental molecular biological science. This situation does well to give our work the interdisciplinarity that's of great advantage to our research while maintaining our autonomy, to say nothing about our sanity and that of our students and post-docs. Our scientific relationship started with Georges tutoring me in chemistry, mathematics, and physics and me helping edit his papers. I still learn from him, but these days, the tables have turned, and I'm his tutor in molecular biology and, most recently, RNA science as an official pro bono consultant on his federal and industrial RNA grants. RNA may seem odd for a chemical engineer, but during the COVID-19 pandemic, he turned his attention to purifying messenger RNA for vaccines.

I am reminded of a multi-investigator, interdisciplinary grant awarded to Georges twenty years ago by the NSF, on which I was a co-investigator. The work conducted under this NSF award is a great example of the pitfalls and triumphs of honest and productive interdisciplinary collaboration. It was focused on inteins, which are a little like introns, but they're made of protein, not RNA. Whereas I was interested in the molecular genetics and evolution of inteins, Georges became fascinated by their chemistry and potential utility. The title of the four-year grant was "Inteins as Nanoswitches for Biotechnology." The co-investigators on the NSF grant application included scientists from both our institutions (I was still at Wadsworth Center at the time): a biochemist, chemical engineer, molecular modeler, crystallographer, geneticist, NMR spectroscopist, and quantum mechanist. Wow!

Our first meeting was exciting—we were pleased to be funded—but soon after our celebration, we descended into disillusionment. Although we succeeded in impressing the NSF reviewers, we each didn't know what the other was talking about or which end was up. This felt very discouraging. As we were mired in ambiguity and uncertainty at these monthly meetings, it soon became clear we first needed to learn one another's vocabularies. We desperately clung to threads of common understanding, not knowing where they would lead. I am reminded of an editorial in *Science* magazine by Phil Sharp and Bob Langer, two friends of ours at MIT, in which they contend that, "Although a deep disciplinary background remains vital, a robust cross-disciplinary education is essential, too. Researchers need to learn a kind of *convergence creole* to help them communicate across disciplinary lines and then to become fully *multilingual*."[31]

After learning new scientific languages and feeling comfortable in areas that initially seemed impenetrable, Georges, I, and all our creative co-investigators brainstormed and did a combination of experimental and computational work that resulted in the publication of many papers, most in areas beyond our initial comfort zones.

---

31   Phillip A. Sharp and Robert Langer, "Promoting Convergence in Biomedical Science," *Science* 333, no. 6042 (July 2011): 527, https://doi.org/10.1126/science.1205008.

We published papers in biochemistry, chemistry, theoretical physics, genetics, chemical engineering, and protein structure. We also expanded our basic science into explorations of biotechnological applications and using inteins as targets to develop novel antibiotics to overcome the drug-resistance problem in bacteria and fungi. Although the grant was first funded in 2003, we still meet periodically with a group that stretches far beyond "across the river." Our students, post-docs, and colleagues have fanned out into industry and academia around the country and the world, from India to Israel. It's a great shared joy for us to see them flourish and establish international outposts of our science. At a recent multinational intein workshop with eight speakers from Canada, Germany, Israel, and the US, half the presenters were our protégés, a great source of pride.

HONORARY DOCTORATES, UCT, 2019: My lifelong partnership with Georges has included many professional collaborations. In 2019, we both received honorary doctorates from our alma mater, University of Cape Town.

This chapter has mostly been about Georges's and my work collaborations, but of course, I can't resist describing some of our domestic partnership as well. Collaboration is at the core of making complex lives that involve professional activities and domestic responsibilities possible. Indeed, it's been argued from evolutionary and economic standpoints that collaboration between the sexes is necessary to raise humans through the protracted period of brain development until independence.[32] But a word of caution: As I teach in my "Resilience Training" course, relationships are like bridges, in constant need of repair or they collapse. Georges's and my partnership is no exception. We need to accommodate mood swings and different philosophies regarding sharing, child-rearing, and even dishwasher loading.

Although usually subject to fewer rules, domestic collaborations are at least as important as professional partnerships for living a full and satisfying life, and the need for *some* rules definitely exists. Sheryl Sandberg, formerly the chief operating officer of Facebook, now Meta, and the mother of two children, advises choosing a partner who will support your ambitions, not only by encouragement but by doing half the work at home.[33] Recall, Sheryl was married to the late Dave Goldberg, an executive with Yahoo and later CEO of SurveyMonkey. The couple frequently discussed being in a shared-earning/shared-parenting marriage.

I agree with Sheryl but also know that doing half the housework doesn't have to mean fifty-fifty on cooking, shopping, laundry, and so on; rather, I believe in sharing the load and dividing the labor fifty-fifty not just arbitrarily but based on which chores each partner is best at and most fit their particular lifestyle and talents. I was the early bird, so it made sense for me to do the morning chores, like packing the kids' lunches, which they frequently traded for less wholesome fare and then complained the rich kids had their sand-

---

[32] Paul Seabright, *The War of the Sexes: How Conflict and Cooperation Have Shaped Men and Women from Prehistory to the Present* (Princeton University Press, 2012).

[33] Sheryl Sandberg, *Lean In: Women, Work, and the Will to Lead* (Alfred A. Knopf, 2013).

wiches packaged in plastic Ziplocs, whereas I used the less expensive and environmentally friendlier paper. On the other hand, Georges was the night owl, taking on many evening responsibilities like difficult homework assignments. I've always enjoyed cooking but not changing the diapers, which was his job. I was less engaged with sports, so that became his primary responsibility while I did most of the shopping. Georges was the soccer coach for all three of our sons' teams for many years, including the men's league as they grew older. Interestingly, Georges played rugby, not soccer, in both South Africa and California, but soccer was the emerging sport in the US, so he pivoted. He also did the lawn-mowing, I the planting, and so on. He traveled more than I did, and when he went on a trip, that was my cue to broaden the collaboration to neighbors and nannies to make it all possible. Alas, we had no family support close by to help relieve the burden.

I should pause here to clarify that, as strong as our personal and professional collaborations may be, our relationship is not always smooth and easy. For example, he feels I'm overbearing sometimes, to which his retort is, "Stop trying to control me!" Also, while I feel greatly respected by Georges, don't get me wrong, there's still plenty of "manterrupting," where I am spoken over, and "mansplaining," where I am spoken down to. Also, he can rule the roost unless I decide to have things done the way *I* think is best. And there are those expressions of unconscious bias, like referring to a female leader as "that woman," whereas if they were a man, he would say "your department chair." I point out these "transgressions," but that too can become difficult when it leads to defensiveness rather than a simple, "You're right. I'll pay more attention to that next time." Undoubtedly, these behaviors have no malintent and result from our all being socialized in a highly patriarchal culture, but there's no getting around the fact that they exist. And though it wasn't always plain sailing, the bonus of our domestic arrangement was that our children had the sense of being parented by both their mother and their father and of being supported by a community of caregivers.

The boys now have their own families. They and their wives are working parents, and they make their own rules for collaboration between spouses and available support networks. So, fifty-fifty, or more-or-less fifty-fifty, lives on.

CHAPTER SEVENTEEN

CONVERGENCE CREOLE

Convergence creole, mentioned in the previous chapter, refers to an interdisciplinary mix of approaches undertaken by intellectually diverse scientists who work together to solve a complex problem.[34] Addressing profound scientific challenges, be they in medicine, technology, or space exploration, requires deep integration across disciplines, with convergence of the physical, mathematical, and computational sciences plus engineering and the life sciences. Susan Hockfield, president of MIT, noted of this convergence revolution, "Physicists gave engineers the electron, and they created the IT revolution. Biologists gave engineers the gene, and together they will create the future."[35] That is a very exciting concept to me.

Some years ago, Georges and I decided we wanted to show our appreciation to our universities for supporting our careers with some token or gesture that captured the excitement we experienced at the border of biology and engineering. We also reflected on the success of

---

[34] Sharp and Langer, "Promoting Convergence in Biomedical Science."

[35] Phil Sharp and Susan Hockfield, "Convergence: The Future of Health," *Science* 355, no. 6326 (February 2017): 589, https://doi.org/10.1126/science.aam85.

that NSF intein grant that funded both our institutions. So, we decided to endow a combined lecture series at both RPI and UAlbany that we titled Life at the Interface of Science and Engineering. The intention was to bring together faculty and students at RPI and UAlbany for an intermingling of research communities to collaborate across disciplines in a convergence model by bringing world-renowned scientists to both institutions. The first speaker in the series was our friend and Nobel laureate Tom Cech, who in 2016 gave the inaugural lectures in the areas of RNA and telomerase, the enzyme at the ends of chromosomes, and its role in cancer. You may recall that Tom was also the guy who almost drove me over the edge in the late 1990s when he questioned my contributions to the intron discovery while doing due diligence for my nomination to the National Academy of Sciences. He also hosted Gabi in his lab for J-term (a kind of mini term at universities that happens in January between semesters) when our son was an undergraduate. Tom was great as our first Life at the Interface speaker and set the stage for other illustrious scientists to follow suit. Our students and colleagues loved the opportunity to engage with a Nobel Prize winner, which was very satisfying to us.

The next year, it was Karl Deisseroth, a physician scientist, who visited. We met Karl when he received the prestigious Albany Medical Center Prize for his work on optogenetics, a genetic technique used by neuroscientists to control the activity of nerve cells with light. Karl is a phenomenon, a practicing psychiatrist at Stanford who works at the boundary of molecular biology and bioengineering and recently published *Projections: A Story of Human Emotions* in which he describes the intersectionality of psychiatry and molecular biology.[36] His work is brilliant and just the type of convergence required to solve the intractable problem of how the brain functions to regulate emotions. Literally mind-blowing! Ironically, I missed Karl's lectures at UAlbany and RPI because I was at Four Winds psychiatric hospital at the time suffering through my second major depressive episode. But

---

36   Karl Deisseroth, *Projections: The New Science of Human Emotion* (Random House, 2021).

I was pleased to have him visit me at the hospital. We sat on the lawn between wards, and while Karl spoke, I pulled on blades of grass and sucked on them. We discussed everything from his work with zebra fish as animal models for depression to my condition and hospitalization. Of course, he got it and left me feeling more hopeful than I had in a long while.

LIFE AT THE INTERFACE OF SCIENCE AND ENGINEERING, 2016: The first speaker in the seminar series that Georges and I endowed was Nobel laureate Tom Cech, who is standing behind me, our three sons and Georges by my side. **L to R:** Gabi, Yona, Dave, Marlene, Tom Cech, and Georges.

Then, in 2018, we hosted Frances Arnold, Georges's friend from Caltech, as speaker. I mentioned Frances previously, in the context of spousal partnerships. In the lead-up to Frances's visit, we were pleasantly surprised to learn she was to receive the Nobel Prize in Chemistry. We were thrilled for Frances but a little concerned she would back out given her new spot in the limelight and all the attendant obligations. But sure enough, Frances showed up and delighted audiences on both campuses with her work on improving the performance of enzymes by evolving them in a test tube. The theme of evolving enzymes was continued the following year by David Liu from Harvard University. David's focus is on genome editing proteins, namely CRISPR proteins, which are targeted to a specific location in the genome and change it at will through a programmable RNA sequence.

Then, as frosting on the CRISPR cake, Jennifer Doudna was one of our speakers in 2021, the year after she was corecipient of the Nobel Prize in Chemistry for codiscovering CRISPR technology. I have known Jennifer for decades, since she was a graduate student, and I recognized all the while she was destined for greatness. I need say no more, as Walter Isaacson has already done so in his book about Jennifer, gene editing, "and the future of the human race" called *The Code Breaker*.[37]

Jennifer's visit was virtual because of the COVID-19 pandemic, as was Steve Quake's that same year. Steve invented new DNA sequencing technologies and microfluidic automation that makes it possible to isolate and characterize single cells. He has also pioneered blood tests and other liquid biopsies in diagnostic approaches that are rapidly replacing invasive tests. Imagine diagnosing a genetic defect through a simple blood test by sequencing DNA and RNA rather than an amniocentesis procedure, with a needle poking into the mother's womb, or monitoring organ transplant rejection without invasive surgery. That's what Steve does. Pretty miraculous!

Fortunately, in 2022, we were able to go in person again as the pandemic was being controlled, and appropriately, we had two speakers whose work related to vaccine development. This was the first time we had invited a *pair* of speakers. Bob Langer of MIT and co-founder of Moderna spoke on micro- and nano-technology delivery systems for mRNA therapies at RPI. Bob is one of the guys who coined the term "convergence creole," arguably the world's most celebrated, productive, and famous chemical engineer. The second speaker, Melissa Moore

---

37 Walter Isaacson, *Code Breaker: Jennifer Doudna, Gene Editing, and the Future of the Human Race* (Simon & Schuster, 2021).

of Moderna, spoke the same day at UAlbany on mRNA as medicine. Melissa is an acclaimed molecular biologist and world-class RNA scientist whom I've also known since she was a trainee decades ago. Bob's an Albany native whose mom lived in our neighborhood before moving to Boston, so we go way back, with Georges and Bob being close chemical engineering buddies since the early days.

Bob described lipid nanoparticles that are used to package RNA medicines, whereas Melissa described the forty-three days between receiving the genome sequence of the COVID-19 virus Sars-cov-2 from Wuhan, China, and sending the first vials of mRNA from Moderna to the NIH for the start of clinical trials. What a testament to the value of basic research! That triumph of modern medical science so excited me I had goose bumps all over my body when I first heard the story of those forty-three days. At dinner, when discussing the boon of mRNA vaccines, Melissa estimated that by that point, September 2022, these vaccines had saved more than twenty million lives. Twenty million! And of course, it's more than that today. More goose bumps.

In 2023, we had David Baker of the University of Washington describe his groundbreaking work on predicting how proteins, the essential cellular workhorses, fold, for which he was awarded the Nobel Prize in Chemistry in 2024. Good timing on our part! That same year we turned to someone quite different, Pat Brown. Pat is an esteemed molecular biologist turned environmentalist and the founder of Impossible Foods. During a sabbatical from Stanford, Pat decided creating plant-based meat substitutes would solve one of the most important problems on earth. The title of his talk was "Escape from the Planet of the Cows." Amusing title but deadly serious. For 2025, Nobel Laureate Phil Sharp, the second of the two convergence creole guys, is speaking, bringing to five the number of Nobelists in the Life at the Interface series in its first ten years.[38] Imagine the

---

38 Andrea Korte, "AAAS to Host 10th Anniversary Life at the Interface of Science + Engineering Lecture," AAAS, February 11, 2025, https://www.aaas.org/news/aaas-host-10th-anniversary-life-interface-science-engineering-lecture.

excitement among trainees and faculty alike to mingle with these luminaries and to hear about these profoundly important discoveries, and from the horses' mouths no less. We look forward to having more scientific superstars visit in the coming years to interact with our faculty and students and getting the locals to interact with one another and make convergent science happen.

CHAPTER EIGHTEEN

WOMEN SUPPORTING WOMEN

The formative years of my life were spent surrounded by women: my mom, Oma, Bessie, and all the girls at Good Hope. Female friendships have been critical to me and often last decades, with new female friendships forming all the time. The Good Hope girls are scattered around the world now, but we still maintain contact and meet whenever the opportunity arises in South Africa, Israel, or Europe. Some are in Australia, and they get together there too, but I've never been down under.

My dearest female friends in Albany are a mix: some soccer moms of the past, some spouses of male faculty, some neighbors. But we're all very close, and it was thirty years ago that we started a gathering called "Group." This was at the time that a now-famous constellation of women scientists in the San Francisco Bay Area created a gathering also called Group to help one another deal with the difficulties of their complex careers. The women in the Albany Group, however, were artists, poets, psychologists, a school superintendent, a music librarian, a professor of history, and only one other scientist. Over the last thirty years, we've lost several members to relocation (this was before the age of meeting remotely), one to death (heartbreaking for us), and one to dementia. Two women joined ten years ago, including the one other scientist. We were all highly connected to one another. So, it was always sad to see members go. In the early 2000s, one of the women, Judy Frangos, a friend since our soccer-mom days, moved to Istanbul to become a music librarian. Georges and I flew over to Turkey shortly thereafter to see how she had settled in and have her show us around Istanbul. She eventually returned to the US, but during the COVID-19 pandemic, several of us moved away from Albany, me included, so now we meet by Zoom. We talk about everything except our sex lives.

When we first started Group, we each described our parents, our relationships with them and our siblings, and the circumstances of our childhoods. The idea was to give each other an intimate basis on which to interact. With that foundation, each woman brings a short topic to discuss each month. We focus on those in greatest need or on celebrating an accomplishment, like a new painting, a recent sculpture, a poetry reading, or a science prize. Problem-solving is often high on the agenda as we deal with issues in the workplace or in our personal lives. We discuss our children, our siblings, aging, illness, our triumphs, and our tragedies, all in great detail. But we also share our more frivolous passions, like which clothes are worth buying, which books we're reading, which movies we recommend, and which cultural events are not to be missed. Politics are big too, with all of us leaning to the left. Attending Group every month is important to all of us, and when there are special circumstances, we'll meet more frequently, such as when I was struggling through my depressions and needed to thwart my sense of isolation. To illustrate the importance of Group, one evening Georges and I were invited to have dinner with Salman Rushdie, who was visiting the New York State (NYS) Writers Institute at UAlbany. That conflicted with a Group meeting, so, to the amazement of some, Georges went to the Rushdie dinner alone. As an interesting aside, just a few years later, the writer was invited to a similar visit at a nonprofit educational institution, also in upstate New York, and was brutally stabbed.

ISTANBUL, around 2000: My soccer-mom friend Judy Frangos, also a founding member of the Albany Group, went to work in Turkey, so I went to visit. Judy **(L)** and Marlene **(R)** beside the Bosphorus.

In the book *Every Other Thursday*, Ellen Daniell describes the female Bay Area scientists from the other, more famous Group, including several friends who are also members of the National Academy of Sciences.[39] The San Francisco Group collaborates in bimonthly gatherings, every other Thursday, also to provide problem-solving and emotional support. They help each other navigate career challenges or other difficulties, providing practical solutions. For example, there's a "to-don't" list for when you're feeling overwhelmed. A friend and colleague at University of California San Francisco, Christine

---

39 Ellen Daniell, *Every Other Thursday: Stories and Strategies from Successful Women Scientists* (Yale University Press, 2008).

Guthrie, was one of the founders of Group and credits it with the successful launch of her career in a hostile, male-dominated work environment after a suicide attempt and psychiatric hospitalization. Unfortunately, we lost Christine to breast cancer a couple years ago. Present at her memorial symposium were sorrowful Nobel laureates alongside grieving members of Group. Another Group friend at UCSF, Carol Gross, tells me they're still meeting biweekly and that Group remains a great source of strength.

Although I've had many female allies throughout my life, there were also female detractors. This was in part due to the unconscious bias women harbor against other women and in part blatant mistreatment rooted, I suspect, in insecurity and jealousy.[40] I felt this very strongly, as described earlier, when I was a post-doc at the Hebrew University and also during some of my years at Wadsworth Center. However, I realized when I left Wadsworth that I had a powerful support system of women scientists there who were both collaborators and friends. These included Lori Flaherty, who took me under her wing when I was about to be fired, as well as several of the women I hired when I took on an administrative role at Wadsworth in the early 1990s. After my dear friend Lori passed away, I was close to Joan Curcio and Kathleen McDonough (both among the local collaborators mentioned above) as well as Arlene Ramsingh and a handful of other Wadsworth scientists. It was therefore bittersweet for all of us when I was preparing to move across town to UAlbany, and so we decided to form the Women of Wadsworth group, WoW, which I mentioned previously in Chapter Nine.

WoW meets irregularly, sometimes in person at someone's home or for a drink after work on a warm summer's day. We also sometimes meet by Zoom, as WoW too has spread across the country, from Berkeley to Miami. I see WoW as "Group Light" when compared with the Albany and Bay Area clusters. Gatherings are less intense

---

40 Lelia Gowland, "The Unconscious Bias Women Have Against Women," *Forbes*, June 25, 2018, https://www.forbes.com/sites/leliagowland/2018/06/25/the-unconscious-bias-women-have-against-women/.

but supportive nonetheless, and members always have one another's backs. So, when I found myself on the UAlbany, SUNY campus in 2011, I missed the Wadsworth women and the bonds we had formed. It also occurred to me there were few female role models in STEM on campus and little in the way of friendships among female faculty, post-docs, and grad students. This vacuum of support for women made me feel sorrowful and isolated and motivated me to fill the void.

In pondering what I wanted to create on the UAlbany campus, I began thinking about my mom. As my role model, she always somehow managed to instill in me the belief there was nothing I couldn't achieve if I really put my mind to it. It's because of her that I carry that important perspective and confidence with me—my hope is my children and students do too—and I have a need to share it. My mom's industriousness alongside her nurturing spirit underlies my need to provide good scientific role models who live balanced lives to inspire our next generation of female students, post-docs, faculty, and other professionals. They need to have the sense that it *can* be done and they can do it.

When I was elected to the National Academy, I vowed to make a difference and recognized I could maximize my impact with *female* scientists, who need it most. I also saw the need for institutional support of women at both personal and policy levels. I went to see then-dean Elga Wulfert, who had hired me, and together, we started the female faculty Women in Science and Health group, WISH.[41] Through regular meetings, WISH promotes scientific networking and provides skill-building opportunities for students, post-docs, and faculty in STEM with the goal of achieving gender equity and work–life integration. For example, we host an annual essay competition open to female and male students and post-docs on "Excellence at the Intersection of Science and Life," offering both monetary prizes and giving the trainees the opportunity to publicly present their win-

---

41 Women in Science and Health (WISH), University of Albany, accessed November 21, 2024, https://www.albany.edu/women-science-health.

ning essays on weaving together their scientific and extracurricular lives. Female STEM student organizations also affiliate with WISH, allowing us to provide both mentoring and financial support. We have sponsored the campus chapter of Scientista, a national women's graduate student group, and a local UAlbany graduate student group, STEM NOW, which stands for Nourishing Opportunities for Women. It's extremely gratifying to see the confidence radiating from the STEM NOW trainees, at least some of which I attribute to peer support and mentoring from WISH. It was also heartening to hear from one of my last graduate students, Cathleen Green Schiraldi, now a staff scientist at Regeneron and a happy mom, that she has formed a women's group to support her colleagues in the industrial setting.

At WISH, we also work on trying to effect systemic change to support working women in the way I experienced in Israel, with a more generous safety net, such as extending the tenure clock and providing parental leave as well as recommending good childcare opportunities. Such transformation has to happen both individually and institutionally. I tell the female graduate students who wish to have children to go for it and that if they work hard, creatively, and with the right support systems, they, like me, will be better mothers *and* better scientists for their efforts. The same is true of fathers.

Of course, I'm well aware of the motherhood penalty, where working moms are handicapped relative to women without children in pay, advancement, and even perceived competence.[42] There is no doubt that sometimes having a child or children can come at the cost of a woman's career, particularly if she has little support, but this definitely doesn't have to be the case. Which is why it's so important women get the help they need to have the careers and families they want, whatever that looks like for them. Certainly, with healthy children and the right support systems, the rewards of the working mom can far outweigh small sacrifices in pay or delays in work progress. None-

---

42 Almond, Cheng, and Machado, "Large Motherhood Penalties in US Administrative Microdata."

theless, we need to work on eradicating the motherhood penalty so moms are not disadvantaged by having children.

As we see adjustment of the tenure clock to accommodate family needs and exceptional circumstances like the COVID-19 pandemic and we also see greater tolerance of work from home, the hope is the lot of mother–scientists will become easier. WISH has certainly provided a good resource for women in STEM. In addition to improving the campus climate and increasing awareness of unconscious bias, WISH recruits male allies to help us in our work. We take male participation seriously and encourage support for the fathers of our children so they can contribute to childcare without sacrificing *their* careers. Indeed, Anne-Marie Slaughter, a Princeton professor of international law, while working for the State Department, contended at the World Economic Forum in Davos, Switzerland, in 2014 and discussed in subsequent interviews that if society freed men to spend their time as they chose, many would focus on family and other loved ones.[43] She also draws a direct relationship between a woman's ability to succeed and her husband's willingness to take on domestic duties.

The WISH leadership has formed a tight-knit group over the years, with interdepartmental relationships that are both academically and socially valuable. There is a lot of behind-the-scenes chitchat about personal issues, be they university politics, like an ornery faculty member, or family dilemmas, like how to deal with troublesome children. And, of course, policies like maternity leave and benefits for both women and men are a primary concern. There is also a cohort of male allies (we call them male ambassadors), who occupy seats of power at the university and help WISH as we strive to attain gender equality. Supportive men are a key element to WISH's success.

---

43 Anne-Marie Slaughter, "Anne-Marie Slaughter's Vision for Women, Men, Work, and Family," interview by *Knowledge at Wharton Podcast*, November 5, 2015, https://knowledge.wharton.upenn.edu/podcast/knowledge-at-wharton-podcast/anne-marie-slaughters-vision-for-women-men-work-and-family-2/.

PROJECT SAGES, 2023: Leadership of SAGES and award recipients. **L to R:** Cecilia Levy, Sujata Murty, Edelgard Wulfert, Aubrey Hillman, Marlene Belfort, Provost Carol Kim, Melinda Larsen, Sweta Vangaveti, Gabriele Fuchs, Cara Pager, Chinwe Ekenna, Betty Lin, and Haruka Takayama.

WISH has become a great support group for our campus women in STEM and provided a springboard for Elga, two other WISH Women, and me to secure an NSF grant under their ADVANCE initiative.[44] The grant points out that family formation, marriage, and childbirth are main reasons for women in STEM to leave the workforce between receipt of their PhD and achieving tenure. This is what I have been struggling to remedy for decades now, to accommodate the dual role of women and men who are caretakers, especially early in their careers, when long hours need to be committed to laboratories and fieldwork and children are young. These can also be important considerations later, when elder-care responsibilities may mount. We were therefore thrilled when our million-dollar NSF Project SAGES grant (Striving to Achieve Gender Equity in STEM) was funded, with Elga spearheading the effort.[45]

Our university president, Havidán Rodríguez, is the principal investigator on the SAGES grant, giving the award the clout to be taken seriously campus wide by male and female faculty alike. SAGES is also consistent with the strategic priority of our campus to diversify our STEM faculty. This award helps accelerate our progress toward creating

---

44 "Advance: Organizational Change for Gender Equity in STEM Academic Professions," U.S. National Science Foundation, accessed January 7, 2025, https://new.nsf.gov/funding/opportunities/advance-advance-organizational-change-gender-equity-stem-academic.

45 Project SAGES, University of Albany, accessed November 21, 2024, https://www.albany.edu/sages.

a faculty that more closely mirrors our highly diverse undergraduate student population, which is described further in the following chapter. SAGES provides research funds to female faculty and also works on improving the campus climate. One funding program awards seed grants to encourage scientific collaboration with scientists, male or female, on our campus or nationally. The idea is to generate data toward successful applications for external grants. Another SAGES program funds female faculty to recruit external sponsors who are experts in their field to support and mentor them and assist with networking beyond the UAlbany campus. These young women are themselves forming a cohort, and one hopes as their careers mature, they will eventually step into leadership roles for the next generation of women in STEM.

Georges sometimes talks to me about my close female friendships, noting with some yearning that male groups are less common. Of course, he has many friends and colleagues with whom he enjoys a strong camaraderie, but without the sense of intimacy that characterizes my relationships with my close women friends. Our son Gabi, with tongue in cheek, calls this the passing of the patriarchy. Yona, on the other hand, has formed a men's book club that meets regularly, resulting in deep relationships with a bunch of like-minded male friends.

The women in my family are also a tight-knit sisterhood. My two sisters-in-law, Rene, a teacher, and Ethel, a museum docent, are my best friends. I am also close to my three daughters-in-law, Mandy, Sara, and Erin, and their moms and sisters (another couple of doctors and a dentist). Recall the title of this book! Family gatherings can sometimes feel like medical conventions (and sometimes like the Jewish holiday meal in *Annie Hall*, with lots of gabbing and interruptions). I also have a niece named Lisa, a journalist to whom I'm exceptionally close (she read the first draft of this book for me). But we also have two nieces, one on each side of the family, who are estranged from their parents and from us. I find the personal loss of these two young women whom I love dearly heartbreaking, but I also feel bad for them, forfeiting the opportunities they would have being part of this clan of loving and impressive women (and their magnificent men).

CHAPTER NINETEEN

BUILDING DIVERSE COMMUNITIES

I come to my work in the equity space in part through the love I felt for Bessie, the African maid who helped raise me; in part through my white conscience in response to the injustices of Apartheid; in part through the pain I feel on behalf of Black and brown people in this country; in part through my own feeling of otherness; and in part through the intersectionality between my work on behalf of women in science and people of color. That intersectionality drove a series of panel discussions titled Women Collaborating for Inclusion sponsored by WISH that were aimed at providing successful role models for our faculty and graduate students of color. This is regularly by far the best attended of our WISH events.

Interestingly, I do some of this work in collaboration with my white South African colleague Cara Pager, a virologist in our department. Sometimes, we struggle to find the right words to discuss matters of race. Is it Blacks or African Americans or people of color? Is it Latino/Latina or Latinx? So, we are learning the correct vocabulary and how to navigate these waters, feeling that as white women we're not quite credentialed to do the work, but we're passionate about doing it anyway. Again, by holding hands, this time across diverse racial groups, we *are* able to make a difference in fighting for equity among all races.

One of our first panelists in the Women Collaborating for Inclusion series was a woman in STEM, of Dominican heritage, who has much to teach in terms of diversifying a campus community in her university leadership and administrative roles. She is also known for her academic excellence, as a full professor in one of the top-ten departments in the country. By all accounts, she is a star who obtained her bachelor and PhD degrees from Ivy League universities. This outstanding scientist is married to an impressive African American businessman, the father of their children. One might assume this successful couple is immune to the racism that plagues our country. But she has confided in me and expressed in the panel that she is sometimes stopped while jogging in her suburban neighborhood with such questions as, "Are you lost?" Microaggressions aside, she is grateful every time her husband arrives back home safely after a quick trip to the neighborhood grocery store. This is how the *stars* of communities of color live; one can only imagine the indignities and hardships of those who live on the margins.

More than 40 percent of our undergraduates at UAlbany identify as Black or Latina/o, a number of which I am proud, given my education in Apartheid South Africa where more than 95 percent of the students at UCT were white and a disproportionate number were men. However, one of our problems on campus is the poor graduation rates of STEM students, particularly those of color. So, in 2016, I visited the Meyerhoff Scholars Program at the University of Maryland, Baltimore County (UMBC), which has been at the forefront of increasing diversity among students pursuing a PhD in STEM. The program's success is built on focused attention on young scholars of color who collaborate in a tightly knit learning community and encourage each other's success. However, the program is expensive. UMBC benefited from the vision of a local businessman with a major endowment from the Meyerhoff family. Therefore, we realized if we wanted to be serious in promoting the success of our underrepresented students, we needed to explore funding possibilities.

Howard Hughes Medical Institute (HHMI) was piloting Meyerhoff-type programs at Pennsylvania State and the University of North Carolina. I attended a workshop at HHMI headquarters in Chevy Chase, Maryland, to learn more. Although there was no chance of securing funds for UAlbany at the time, I registered my interest with the director of education there, and several years later, in 2019, HHMI announced their Driving Change initiative. UAlbany was one of 255 institutions eligible for HHMI funding nationwide, of which one hundred submitted letters of intent. Of those one hundred, thirty-eight, UAlbany among them, were invited to submit full applications based on their readiness to engage in the hard work of cultural change on their campuses. We received pilot funding to conduct a self-study spearheaded by Dr. Rabi Musah, a female, African American professor of chemistry.

Rabi is a dynamo, a successful chemist who had previously been funded by the NSF to boost student achievement, retention, and success in STEM. Sure enough, a team effort led by Rabi over several years was successful in receiving an HHMI Driving Change award in 2022. We were one of only six universities nationwide to receive an initial $2.5 million award to pioneer novel, inclusive approaches to teaching STEM disciplines and create a student-support network to increase retention and graduation rates. The idea was to build a strong peer-mentoring system led by successful students of color, which Rabi has already piloted with an encouraging retention rate.[46] My entire body shivered when we received word we would be funded. I recall only four times previously becoming all goose-bumpy and shivering with excitement: Recently, with the rapid development of the COVID-

---

46 University of Albany, "UAlbany Awarded $2.5M Grant to Pioneer STEM Success Programs," news release, November 2, 2022, https://www.albany.edu/news-center/news/2022-ualbany-awarded-25m-grant-pioneer-stem-success-programs.

19 mRNA vaccine, thirty-five years ago in 1990 when Nelson Mandela was released from prison, then five years before that with the intron discovery, and way back in the 1960s when I was seventeen years old and Georges held my hand for the very first time.

Diversity in our communities is extraordinarily enriching. Different ways of doing things combine to make a whole that is greater than the sum of its parts. Rabi and I sometimes go to coffee together, musing over how these two African women from very different backgrounds, she from Ghana, me from South Africa, have made it in this cutthroat academic world. We conclude that we lived life without many instructions or rules. We were raised as free spirits in charge of our own destinies. We shopped in open-air markets, cooked based on the harvest, concocted recipes, and examined the plants we walked among on our way to school. Indeed, Rabi's successful career in chemistry is based on those very plants, which have led her into disciplines as disparate as forensics and cancer chemotherapy. Living without rules also carries forward into our research originality and creativity in the kitchen. We're not limited by what's prescribed.

We need more Rabis on campus, but how will we compete with the Ivy League for faculty of color? They need Rabis too. To solve this problem, I thought we should create a pipeline from our talented PhD students of color to the faculty. So, Cara, Rabi, and I have implemented a prestigious Graduate Pathway for Scholars (GPS) Program to incentivize PhD students to return to UAlbany as faculty after completing post-doctoral studies at another respected institution. Incentives include an initial monetary award, title of GPS Scholar, targeted mentoring, and affiliation with inclusive UAlbany faculty groups like BILPOC (Black, Indigenous, Latinx, People of Color). The idea is that BILPOC on campus will provide community and be a magnet to attract others "home" as faculty after their post-doctoral stints. The eventual goal is to secure a multimillion-dollar NSF award to sustain the GPS program. We are just at the very beginning of piloting GPS with two STEM departments on campus, biology and chemistry, and are already encouraged by having awarded two GPS fellowships and one honorable mention. They presented recently at a BILPOC symposium—it was pure pleasure to prep them for a talk to a general audience—and did a great job, but of course, the proof will be in the pudding if they are attracted back to UAlbany.

At a recent RNA conference in Singapore, I attended a session on diversity, equity, and inclusion. The panelists were female and male academics of varying skin tones and from different continents. But the panelist who stood out most for me was a young Palestinian graduate student wearing a hijab, Mai Baker from the Hebrew University in Jerusalem. This was before the October 7, 2023 attack that was the start of the war between Israel and Hamas. Mai described her research in RNA science, which she performed with her Israeli collaborators, and an RNA cluster she was forming on the West Bank with her Palestinian friends. Mai captured my imagination, and I wanted to hug her for her courage and allowing me to dare dream about peace in the Middle East. Can we collaborate on RNA science as a bridge to peace? There seems so much more that unites Mai and me, a Palestinian and a Jewish woman, than divides us. The same could be true for collaboration among mathematicians or artists or chefs or musicians or filmmakers or engineers or businesspeople. If there's any hope for peace in this troubled patch of land, and other conflict zones around the world, it needs to come from partnerships in different specialties, showing the politicians the way. This may sound simplistic and idealistic, but it comes from a place deep in my heart.

PART FIVE

THE FOURTH QUARTER

> "The only thing that people regret is that they didn't live boldly enough, that they didn't invest enough heart, didn't love enough."
>
> —TED HUGHES, *LETTERS OF TED HUGHES*

What is the Fourth Quarter? I consider it the last of Erik Erikson's eight life stages. For me, it's the chapter of life after age seventy, a phase often dreaded. But I believe this period of life can actually be one of the most fulfilling. It is also a stage in which one can continue to make a difference in the world, to one's family, friends, colleagues, students, and community, and reap rich rewards. For example, at age seventy, I arranged a wonderful seventy-fifth birthday celebration for Georges with close family and friends overlooking the water on Cape Cod. Then, at seventy-three, the entire family went to Cancun Mexico to celebrate our fiftieth wedding anniversary and I co-organized an international symposium on Mobile Genetic Elements and Genome Plasticity in Santa Fe, New Mexico, which was well attended, highly relevant, and personally satisfying.

GEORGES'S SEVENTY-FIFTH BIRTHDAY PARTY: We had a great time roasting and toasting Georges. Reprinted with permission from Condé Nast.

CELEBRATING OUR FIFTIETH WEDDING ANNIVERSARY, 2017: Here we are, all jumping for joy in Cancun, Mexico. **L to R:** Dave, me, Yona, Strand, Sam, Georges, Nadia, Mandy, Erin, Levi, Zachary, Sara, Sequoia, Gabi and Lincoln. A happy bunch.

Later in life can also be the time in science when you finally get recognized for the entirety of your work over the course of a decades-long career. At seventy-seven, I was really excited to receive a mentoring award from the ASBMB because guiding the next generation means the world to me. Then, receiving the RNA Society's Lifetime Achievement in Science Award at seventy-eight was humbling and a gratifying bookend to my career. Imagine the thrill of receiving an RNA award right after that molecule literally saved the world from COVID-19. I received many congratulatory notes from prominent colleagues from around the world, but it was the joy of the students around me and that of my family that felt most meaningful.

This is a time to look back and reflect upon a life dedicated to science and family and look forward and plan to make up for the sacrifices of your earlier days, when you were consumed by the rigors of work and family life.

CHAPTER TWENTY

LOOKING BACK AT LIFE IN BASIC RESEARCH—THE PRIVILEGE, THE VALUE

I've enjoyed a privileged life indeed, following my passion in science and having my curiosity satisfied in so many ways. All my work has been based on that central dogma of molecular biology that most of you have heard: DNA (the gene) to RNA (the messenger) to proteins (the functional components of cells, like enzymes and building blocks). Testing ideas and hunches is exciting, and although the breakthroughs come in spurts, interrupted by sometimes lengthy periods of frustration and setbacks, discoveries are supremely thrilling—I likened them previously to finding love and giving birth. And better yet, this type of discovery-based research can sometimes result in useful, even lifesaving, practical applications, as we'll see later in this chapter. Layer onto that teaching and training aspiring young scientists, perhaps the greatest privilege of all. Imagine going to work each day and engaging with inquiring young minds, sharing ideas, motivating young colleagues to achieve their fullest potential, watching them grow and mature.

But getting there took a while. As a graduate student at UC Irvine in the 1960s, I decided to work on bacteriophage, called "phage" for short, which are tiny viruses that infect bacteria and gobble up these cells ("phage" comes from the Greek word meaning "to devour"). I had the sense back then that these relatively simple organisms, bacteria and phage (phage can be singular or plural), could tell us multitudes about life, infection, gene function, and evolution, and I spent the rest of my career developing a detailed understanding of these phenomena. In those early days, I discovered the course of a phage infection can be greatly influenced by the status of the bacterial host cell, much like the outcome of a viral infection is determined in part by the genetics of the human host. The title of my PhD thesis, "Involvement of Bacterial Genotype in Bacteriophage Lambda's Decision Between Lysogeny and Lysis," was just a fancy way of saying the genes of the host can influence whether a virus remains dormant in a cell or pops it open; and "lambda" is simply the name of the particular phage I chose to work on. This was likely the world's very first inkling that the outcome of a phage infection can have as much to do with the genetic makeup of the host cell it was infecting as with the virus itself. Imagine the thrill of that discovery as a graduate student, although I doubt I recognized its full importance. This same theme underlies those CRISPR gene-editing elements we hear so much about today, which lurk in bacteria and influence the outcomes of phage infection. More on CRISPR later in this chapter.

I probably already spent too much time in Chapters Eight and Nine telling you about the discovery we made at Wadsworth Center of an interruption in a gene sequence in a different phage, called T4. Not only had we shown that this "intron" existed in phage (at that time, introns were thought only to be found in "higher" organisms, like plants and animals, including humans) but also that they were removed from the RNA in a process called "splicing." Splicing is just like cutting out those unwanted segments of a film and joining the relevant pieces. Joan Steitz, my advocate and friend, who appeared in Chapter Nine, said of this discovery, which I announced at a conference at Cold Spring Harbor Laboratory, "I had not known Marlene prior to the moment in 1984 when she burst upon the RNA processing community with her amazing announcement of self-splicing introns in T4 phage. From the very first, it was clear that anything we would hear from Marlene would be based on immaculate data (whether genetic or biochemical) eloquently presented." I am extremely humbled by these words. As Joan said, these introns are self-splicing RNA enzymes, like those discovered by our friend Tom Cech, as so eloquently described in his recent book *The Catalyst*, which essentially delves into his love affair with RNA.[47]

Keeping our noses to the grindstone, my group then showed that these awesome introns can also move to specific sites in genes. That is, they can behave like mobile genetic elements crashing into DNA. Similar "jumping genes" were first described by Barbara McClintock, working in obscurity a half century ago also at Cold Spring Harbor Laboratory and for which she was awarded the Nobel Prize in Physiology or Medicine in 1983.[48] We showed that the mobile introns perform this remarkable feat of DNA-crashing by carrying with them sequences that code for enzymes that can cut DNA at specific sites. The intron then enters that site of cleavage. These enzymes are called "nucleases" or "DNases." Again, this is not too dissimilar to the CRISPR system, which also functions using a DNase.[49] This new chapter in our story was fascinating, as we worked out molecular pathways where these and other self-splicing introns move from phage to phage and also mobilize within bacteria. Discovery of these amazing jumping introns led to the development of models, bolstered by supporting evidence, for the mechanism of intron evolution that not only is applicable to bacteria and phage but explains enigmatic features of

---

47 Thomas R. Cech, *The Catalyst: RNA and the Quest to Unlock Life's Deepest Secrets* (W. W. Norton & Co., 2024).

48 Evelyn Fox Keller, *A Feeling for the Organism: The Life and Work of Barbara McClintock* (W. H. Freeman, 1983).

49 Martin Jinek et al., "A Programmable Dual RNA-Guided DNA Endonuclease in Adaptive Bacterial Immunity," *Science* 337, no. 6096 (June 2012): 816–821, https://doi.org/10.1126/science.1225829.

vertebrate genes as well.⁵⁰ This work was not only exhilarating but also key to establishing my scientific credibility and stature.

Harkening back to my PhD research, I once again became fascinated by the intricate balance between these mobile elements and their hosts and defined molecular mechanisms where the element is *silenced*, that is, kept from moving.⁵¹ We viewed these mobile introns as little parasites that needed to be kept dormant so as not to kill the very host cell that was providing them sanctuary. But then, mobile elements also need the option to move under conditions of stress that threaten host survival and their own extinction, like starvation. We demonstrated how that happened, again at the molecular level, in work that began at Wadsworth and continued after our move to UAlbany. That work, published in high-profile journals, was editorialized in a way that emphasized its importance and remarked on the creativity of our approaches. So, in addition to the excitement of discovery, there was the added bonus of recognition, which helped the students and post-docs find their next jobs at terrific places and kept the lab well funded by federal grants for years and sometimes a decade at a time.

Meanwhile, as I described in Chapter Sixteen, Georges and I collaborated on inteins, which interrupt important genes needed for bacteria to survive. Rather than splicing at the RNA level, inteins remain stuck in the RNA and are excised from the protein in a process aptly called "protein splicing." Whereas I focused on mechanistic and evolutionary aspects of inteins, Georges helped demonstrate intein utility in biotechnology. A true engineer! He helped develop inteins for protein separations for the pharma industry with the help of our brilliant joint graduate student, David Wood, who trained in both

---

50 Arthur Beauregard, M. Joan Curcio, and Marlene Belfort, "The Take and Give Between Retrotransposable Elements and Their Hosts," *Annual Review of Genetics* 42 (December 2008): 587–617, https://doi.org/10.1146/annurev.genet.42.110807.091549.

51 Colin J. Coros et al., "Global Regulators Orchestrate Group II Intron Retromobility," *Mollecular Cell* 34, no. 2 (April 2009): 250–256, https://doi.org/10.1016/j.molcel.2009.03.014.

chemical engineering and molecular biology.[52] We also identified inteins as novel antimicrobial drug targets. If we can stop protein splicing, we argued, we can kill the intein-containing microbe without harming humans, which don't contain inteins. When the intein remains stuck in an important gene, that can kill the microbe, or at least stop it from causing a productive infection. We thus developed platinum-based lead compounds as potential antibiotics against microbes that cause tuberculosis and nasty fungal diseases.[53]

But what captivated me for years was the notion that inteins could act as switches, turning proteins on and off. After all, inteins can be made to remain in the protein, inactivating it, but when they splice out, voilà: The protein assumes its function, the intein having left without even a trace. If we humans can think it possible and it makes good sense, you better believe nature has already done it. We hammered on this concept for years, and two particularly talented post-docs, Brian Callahan and Chris Lennon, cracked it.[54] Based on bioinformatic, genetic, biochemical, and structural studies, they helped overturn dogma that inteins, which can also be mobile and crash into DNA, are purely useless parasitic elements. They provided several examples of inteins adapting cleverly to the lifestyle of their host cell. Therefore, inteins can regulate protein function in response to environmental cues, such as temperature, oxidative stress, and DNA damage, and provide a potential advantage to their host. Let's use temperature as an example. If there's an intein in an energy-consuming gene that is needed to survive at high temperature, it would be wasteful for the cell to have the protein active at low temperature. This would be much like having the air conditioner running when it's cold outside. But

---

52 David W. Wood et al., "A Genetic System Yields Self-Cleaving Inteins for Bioseparations," *Nature Biotechnololgy* 17 (September 1999): 889–892, https://doi.org/10.1038/12879.

53 Liyun Zhang et al., "Cisplatin Inhibits Protein Splicing, Suggesting Inteins as Therapeutic Targets in Mycobacteria," *Journal of Biological Chemistry* 286, on. 2 (January 2011): 1277–1282, https://doi.org/10.1074/jbc.M110.171124.

54 Brian P. Callahan et al., "Structure of Catalytically Competent Intein Caught in a Redox Trap with Functional and Evolutionary Implications," *Nature Structural & Molecular Biology* 18 (April 2011): 630–633, https://doi.org/10.1038/nsmb.2041; Christopher W. Lennon and Marlene Belfort, "Inteins," *Current Biology* 27, no. 6 (March 2017): R204–R206, https://doi.org/10.1016/j.cub.2017.01.016.

when that cell heats up, the intein splices out such that the protein required for cell survival at elevated temperature becomes functional. Again, the AC is required for our survival only when it is extremely hot. Similarly, there were other eureka moments showing that intein switches can be of tremendous use in shutting different genes on and off, depending on the habitat and lifestyle of a particular organism.

So, you might be wondering, as we did, what the function of introns and inteins in nature is. Are they purely selfish parasites that have learned to invade DNA and persist in cells? Or might they be altruistic, having ingratiated themselves to the cells, making themselves useful and even indispensable? There has been much speculation over the years and debate back and forth. Given what I've said in the preceding paragraph, you already know which side I'm on: I come down clearly in favor of the utility of some of these elements.[55] But, alas, some have denigrated them as genetic "junk." A highly relevant example is the human genome, only 1 to 2 percent of which encodes proteins. What of the protein deserts? Are they useless genetic junk too? Hardly! Increasingly, we're uncovering important functions for the other 98 to 99 percent. It will take decades to ascribe function to all this vast amount of non-protein-coding human DNA, but thanks to the advent of AI coupled with inexpensive genome sequencing and brilliant minds, the function of non-coding DNA is within reach, solving one of the great natural mysteries of our time.

What, you might ask, does this all mean for humanity? Well, many thousands of sequence variants in both protein-coding and protein-non-coding regions are related to human diseases, including some cancers, obesity, Parkinson's disease, and autism, to name a few. In other words, we're that much closer to understanding and finding cures for these serious illnesses.

One way to overcome the disastrous effects of harmful gene variations in DNA, also known as mutations, is using CRISPR gene-editing

---

[55] Marlene Belfort, "Mobile Self-Splicing Introns and Inteins as Environmental Sensors," *Current Opinion in Microbiology* 38 (August 2017): 51–58, https://doi.org/10.1016/j.mib.2017.04.003.

technology. CRISPR, with a DNase enzyme, one of which is called Cas9, can be directed to cut DNA specifically at the mutation site, enabling accurate editing by fixing the DNA where it was cut. There are treatments being developed and clinical trials in progress for blood disorders, diabetes, diseases of the immune system, and HIV/AIDS, among others.[56] Happily, in late 2023, the FDA approved the first CRISPR-based gene therapy to treat a disease of the hemoglobin in red blood cells. This ailment, called sickle cell disease, is devastatingly painful, disproportionately afflicting African Americans. The CRISPR/Cas9 medicine, marketed as Casgevy, is used to edit patients' blood stem cells such that a normal version of hemoglobin is produced, relieving the excruciatingly painful symptoms. Although still a prohibitively expensive treatment, CRISPR technology, based on decades of fundamental research on phage like that which I described above for mobile introns, is providing hope for millions.

I mentioned back in Chapter Seventeen that my friend Jennifer Doudna shared a Nobel Prize in 2020 for codiscovering CRISPR technology.[57] Her corecipient was Emmanuelle Charpentier. They were highly deserving of the prize, but we should not ignore the decades of fundamental research on which their breakthrough gene-editing technology was based. Indeed, the Albany Prize, a $500,000 prize awarded annually since 2001 for exceptional work in medicine and biomedical research, was given to *five* recipients in 2017, including Jennifer and Emmanuelle. The other three were acknowledged mainly for their early basic research on which Jennifer and Emmanuelle's research was based. There have been other prizes for CRISPR discoveries with different constellations of awardees, but I mention the Albany Prize for two reasons. First, I am proud to say I've served on the prize committee since its inception, and we've picked some extraordinary winners, many of whom have gone on to win Nobel

---

56 Hope Henderson, "CRISPR Clinical Trials: A 2024 Update," Innovative Genomics Institute, March 13, 2024, https://innovativegenomics.org/news/crispr-clinical-trials-2024/.

57 Jinek et al., "A Programmable Dual RNA-Guided DNA Endonuclease in Adaptive Bacterial Immunity."

Prizes. Second, there's another wonderful story on the value of basic research involving the Albany Prize.

In 2021, we selected Katalin Karikó, Drew Weissman, and Barney Graham for the Albany Prize for their key roles in accelerating the development of COVID-19 mRNA vaccines. Two years later, Kati and Drew were awarded the Nobel Prize in Physiology or Medicine, their work forming the basis of the Pfizer/BioNTech and Moderna vaccines. But Kati had labored for decades to decipher the secret sauce that allows synthetic mRNA to survive in the human body, making possible within months the rapid manufacture of mRNA vaccines. More generally, the successes of these two companies were based again on a half century of fundamental RNA research. So, not only is it a privilege and a thrill to wake up every morning thinking of the next hypothesis to test and experiment to run but the process can be instrumental in saving tens of millions of lives around the globe. I hope I've convinced you that while we can attempt to devise experiments to help humankind, like trying to develop new antibiotics that target inteins to solve the drug-resistance problem, it's often the un-targeted deep research that is life changing for the masses.

As I sit on my perch in my Fourth Quarter, reflecting on my childhood fascination with nature on land and in the sea in beautiful Cape Town, I am grateful to have caught a glimpse of some of the intricate underpinnings of life at different levels. In the words of Barbara McClintock, I developed, "A feeling for the organism," as I have for the cell, the molecule, and even the atom.[58] I couldn't have imagined, when sitting at that microscope while a student in my teens at UCT, when I wanted to see further, right into those cells, that one day I would. I couldn't have conceived of the thrill of observing the molecules that make cells function, of seeing how they embrace each other, like DNA bound to protein in a tight grip, or the pleasure of collecting data that reflected RNA conducting animated dances in the cell.

I also have been given the gift of sitting on review panels, which,

---

58   Fox Keller, *A Feeling for the Organism*.

despite requiring hard work, give a sneak preview of cutting-edge research that's on the drawing board and about to be funded. There's also the honor of being invited to serve on prize committees, reviewing the very best science on the planet and familiarizing oneself with the breathtaking careers of an array of brilliant scientists. It sometimes feels like adjudicating a dress rehearsal for the Nobel Prize and sometimes like choosing between different flavors of ice cream, chunky chocolate, vanilla crunch, or strawberry velvet. I am grateful for all this but mostly for the freedom to pursue the science of my childhood dreams and gain some deep insights into biological matter and its evolution as well as for the privilege of seeing the value in understanding.

CHAPTER TWENTY-ONE

MAJOR MOVES

In March 2020, at the height of the COVID-19 pandemic, our labs shut down, and we went into remote-working mode. Georges and I, being in the high-risk age demographic, spent much of our time at our home on Cape Cod. We took daily walks on the beach, enjoying the sound of the waves, the smell of the sea, the ripples in the sand, and similar seagulls to the ones we used to see flying overhead on Clifton beach, where we met more than sixty years earlier in Cape Town. Then, we decided we should put our Slingerlands house in New York on the market as soon as it became possible to do so and have our home on Cape Cod become our primary residence. Meanwhile, we sorted through forty-two years of "stuff," most of which was useless, but much had sentimental value. For example, I was struck by a quote above my desk by Nelson Mandela from 1964, the year he was sentenced to life in prison: "I have cherished the ideal of a democratic and free society in which all persons live together in harmony and equal opportunities. It is an ideal which I hope to live for and to achieve. But if need be, it is an ideal for which I am prepared to die."[59] You can take the girl out

---

[59] Nelson Mandela, Rivonia Trial speech, April 20, 1964, https://www.nelsonmandela.org/news/entry/i-am-prepared-to-die.

of South Africa, but you can't take South Africa out of the girl. When we eventually moved out of Playfields, I took the browned newspaper clipping and pasted it above my desk at the Cape.

While rummaging through years of accumulated keepsakes, I spent hours reading every note any of the kids ever wrote me, poring over their artwork, browsing their report cards, and fingering their baby teeth that had been left for the tooth fairy. The flashbacks were so vivid it was as if I could smell their sweaty soccer clothes, hear their noisy friends, and feel the vibrations of their rowdy parties. But I also recalled some shenanigans that went over the top, stressing Georges and me out. One of the boys peeled away from his classmates during a school trip to New York City and was nowhere to be found, and another jumped a freight train that ran next to our yard, arriving in the next town to be met by police. Thankfully, shortly thereafter the tracks were converted to a popular nine-mile rail trail that runs from the port of Albany on the Hudson River toward the picturesque Helderberg Mountains. Back in the train-track days, I embraced the phrase "healthy and happy" as a mantra, something to calm my nerves when the boys pulled their pranks and made choices we didn't like. I use it to this day when they go in a direction I'm unsure of, saying to myself that if they're healthy and happy, that's all that matters, and I must let it go. Healthy and happy. Healthy and happy.

In fact, as I was sorting through all those keepsakes and memorabilia and reflecting on what newbies we were when we first arrived in Albany—inexperienced parents, naive scientists, transplanted children—I couldn't help but marvel at how well it all worked out. And how with time, I overcame most of my insecurities as a mother and a scientist. Both our careers, mine and Georges's, progressed, his more steadily than mine. And as the years passed, the children thrived, went off to college then grad school, and married, and we became grandparents. I felt both sad that our time at Playfields, where we had raised our boys, was coming to an end and excited to be moving on with the deep satisfaction of a life well lived.

In September of that first COVID-19 year, prices in the real-estate market started trending up again since being shut down at the start of the pandemic. Our house sold immediately. As always, I hired help, a wonderful organizer who kept me on task and away from my constant reveries with each item I touched; she had me sort things into boxes labeled "Trash," "Cape," "Apartment," "Grassroots Givers," and "Friend Giveaway." I loved donating items and giving others away to friends as we downsized into an apartment across from the UAlbany campus. The "SOLD" sign went up outside the house next to the Playfields sign, exactly where the children waited for their school bus. I had recollections of them asking neighborhood moms jogging by, many the wives of doctors, why they didn't have jobs (because their own mom didn't ever have the time to jog!). Times have changed and life is good; in our current world, the wives *are* the doctors.

The second huge transition was ending my research career and closing my lab. Again, it was an agonizing decision: What would I do if I wasn't writing grants and papers, meeting with my students and post-docs, and heading off to conferences and study sections? Perhaps more importantly, who would I be if not a respected researcher?

Also in the mix was the fact that science itself was changing. Or rather, the way that people *did science* was changing. I resonate with an essay written by Nobel laureate Paul Nurse in *Nature* in 2021 in which he said, "Rather often, I go to a research talk and feel drowned in data. It is as if speculation about what the data mean and the discussion of ideas are not quite proper."[60] Yes, the data. All the high-throughput technologies are churning out volumes of data, including in my own lab. Manipulating the storm of numbers and map positions of gene coordinates became a big deal for me. Like Paul, I was more in tune with the more nuanced and hypothesis-driven science and less prepared for the heavy-duty computation. This made my decision to close the lab easier. And when I thought about the question of who I would be if not a researcher, I soon found my answer. Turns out, I could still

---

60 Paul Nurse, "Biology Must Generate Ideas as Well as Data," *Nature* 597, no. 7876 (September 13, 2021): 305, https://doi.org/10.1038/d41586-021-02480-z.

be incredibly valuable as a senior member of the academic community, helping others get things done—everything from nominating deserving colleagues for awards and helping them gain membership to scientific societies to assisting with securing grants and remaining on editorial boards of journals. There was also work to do for WISH and Project SAGES and for fostering diversity among faculty and equity among students. Also, I still do external advisory work for the Marine Biological Laboratory in Woods Hole, now run by the University of Chicago. And, of course, I'm still a mom to both my biological and "molecular" children, as I call my trainees and mentees.

When I attended a PhD-student recruitment event and no longer needed to compete for graduate students, I felt relieved. I knew I had made the right decision. But when my last remaining PhD student, Justin Waldern, defended his thesis in February 2021, I was filled with trepidation. It felt like the last of the children was leaving home. As I worked with him on his final paper for publication, the findings seemed disparate to me and put me in a low mood, but we stuck with it, muddled through, and, after a struggle, came up with an elegant contribution to the field. This experience reminded me of the words of mathematician Andrew Wiles, "It's groping and probing and poking, and some bumbling and bungling, and then a switch is discovered, often by accident, and the light is lit."[61] Once again, we muddled through until a cohesive story emerged from those incongruent results. But the fact that I had been feeling down during that process of bumbling and bungling gave me pause. Might feeling low be a springboard to a creative synthesis of results and ideas? If feeling down is really a form of mild depression, might depression be adaptive and selected for to provide the impetus for the next breakthrough? The answer, I learned, was yes. In fact, there's an entire body of literature on depression and adaptation, and thankfully, I will now have the time to read some of it.[62]

---

61 Stuart Firestone, *Ignorance: How it Drives Science* (Oxford University Press, 2012).

62 Randolph M. Nesse, "Is Depression an Adaptation?," *Archives of General Psychiatry* 57, no. 1 (January 2000):14–20, https://doi.org/10.1001/archpsyc.57.1.14.

After helping Justin with his final paper, I wrote to tell all my former trainees, about seventy-five of them, that I'd be closing my lab and moving on, offering up microbial samples and reagents they might need. I told them about Georges and me, our three sons and seven grandchildren, and even my intention to write a memoir. Their feedback was heartwarming. Our lab was clearly an important training ground for them, one in which they matured and developed as scientists. Much as my biological children fill me with a sense of pride, my molecular children keep giving back, with their visits, successes, and growth into valuable professionals. They have become respected scientists, valued supervisors in government laboratories, deans and provosts at major universities, and high-level scientists at biotechnology companies. As much as I interact with my own children, I still collaborate with former trainees, having recently edited two compendia of papers in two different journals with former post-docs. It continues to be a win–win interaction for us: me giving them the opportunities that I was offered and boosting their careers and them keeping me engaged and up to date, *with it*, so to speak.

It took an entire year for me to clear my plate after closing the lab, writing final reports to funding agencies, sending out manuscripts for publication, helping secure jobs for the last of the post-docs, and working with my lab manager of twenty years, Matt Stanger, on the enormous physical task of closing the lab. Once again, it felt good to hand off valued items, in this case equipment and supplies, to people I care about. But the process was not without moments of regret. For example, deciding how to indicate on my lab website that the lab had closed was a little like planning my own funeral or writing my own obituary. Then, starting a Dropbox folder for "Recipes" above "Reviews" gave me pause, sounding the alarm bell of transition from serious writing to frivolous cooking. Also, when I started a folder under K titled "Knitting" just before L, "Life Sciences Research Building," which I still lead, I was rattled. Contemplating the shift from the high-powered directing of a scientific operation to the hum-drum handiwork of aging, both activities I genuinely enjoy, seemed jarring, so I will do the phase change slowly.

LYDIA CONTRERAS: Lydia and I became friends when she was a post-doc in my lab (left, 2009), and our collaboration continues to this day. She is now an endowed full professor at University of Texas at Austin and an associate dean. The picture on the right is from 2021.

Although science and academia still occupy a large part of me and remain a stabilizing guidepost, I'm no longer tied to a lab, and I now have the time to indulge myself a little, to read the Sunday paper section by section, to go shopping with my grandchildren, to cook from recipes (of course, with my own modifications) instead of throwing together meals, to exercise, and to write this book. This is a new type of writing for me, which feels both empowering and scary. It also seems self-indulgent and different from anything I've ever done, making me a novice and without the customary feedback from students, colleagues, and journal editors. I have no guardrails, no safeguards, so it's like I'm walking naked into the world. That's both intimidating and exciting. This type of new activity, as I move through the Fourth Quarter and know that I'm still growing, is emboldening, giving me the confidence to experiment with other new activities I've dreamed about but never had time for, maybe pottery, maybe pickleball, maybe writing some poetry or a book with Georges, or perhaps with Rabi, and definitely doing something useful in the social justice space. I take heart from the words of James D. Watson, the codiscoverer of the DNA double helix, "It's necessary to be slightly underemployed if you are to do something significant."[63]

---

[63] James D. Watson, *The Double Helix: A Personal Account of the Discovery of the Structure of DNA* (Atheneum, 1968).

And although Jim Watson has been discredited for his views on race and intelligence, I think he's right on this one. So, my hope is the relative freedom from work will unleash some creative juices rather than encourage me to lie around on the beach.

My son Gabi and I were chatting recently, and we each asked what the other was doing. When it came my turn to respond, I couldn't possibly get up to his level of clinical trials for developing neuropsychiatric drugs, but I answered with my realization that time mixed with a combination of clout and kindness can be very powerful. I was in the process of nominating a colleague for a prestigious award, helping another revise a grant application, and knitting a throw for Gabi's son Lincoln, who is about to go to college. People in this age group can be philanthropic with their money, their time, and their talents, and it is highly satisfying.

I am reminded of a book by Sara Lawrence-Lightfoot, a sociologist and professor of education at Harvard, titled *The Third Chapter*. It's about the twenty-five years after the age of fifty. Although my Fourth Quarter begins at seventy, what this chapter has in common with her book is an exploration of the penultimate stage of life, that period between midlife and old age. As we live longer, so midlife creeps up in years. Lightfoot, who is roughly the same age as I, claims, "The Third Chapter can be the most transformative time in our lives, just as long as we have the courage to challenge the ageist stereotypes, the creativity to resist the old cultural norms, the curiosity to be open to new learning and the adventurousness to pursue new passions and experiences."[64] Her book was first published in 2009, but I heard Sara speak recently at the Falmouth Forum in Woods Hole, and her energy in person fifteen years on was as compelling as the message of her book.

So, challenging the ageist stereotypes, using my time philanthropically, and working to remain healthy need to be part of how I live now.

---

64 Sarah Lawrence-Lightfoot, *The Third Chapter: Passion, Risk, and Adventure in the 25 Years After 50* (Sarah Chrichton Books, 2009), xii.

CHAPTER TWENTY-TWO

THE ONE LAST BIAS

Whereas Asian societies tend to respect their elders, who are revered in old age, Western societies are not so inclined, and rather than honoring senior citizens, they often discriminate against them. This kind of ageism by our youth-obsessed culture is a growing problem as our lifespans increase and the world's climate becomes less and less hospitable. We baby boomers in our Fourth Quarter experience the bias, conscious or unconscious, everywhere, in the workplace, at the supermarket, at the gym, and when the plumber visits us at home and asks if there's a young man in the house for him to speak to. Or when the gardener looks right past me and addresses Georges, like I'm nonexistent. Were these guys being ageist or sexist? Or both? How is it that men become more handsome with age, but women become little old ladies?

To prevail over ageism, I exercise, take good care of myself, and try as much as possible to engage in intergenerational activities (the subject of the next chapter) with my students, children, grandchildren, and neighbors. With my students, we try to build inclusivity and talk science; with my children, I plan get-togethers, argue politics, and laugh; with my grandchildren, I ride bikes and plumb their interests;

and with my neighbors, I do yoga and get the local gossip. I love to see those young minds and strong bodies at work and play. Also, I am on the steering committee for the development of a Center for Healthy Aging at UAlbany to harness the expertise of our nine schools and colleges, including science and engineering programs, public health and social welfare departments, and regional medical centers, to drive public policy and research advances. Basically, the goal is to use science to understand the nature of aging and extend the healthy, active years of life through providing the appropriate social and infrastructure support systems. This kind of interdisciplinary engagement is both stimulating and necessary to overcome the disabilities and the stigma that arise with age.

Although I'm upbeat about the Fourth Quarter, it began with several setbacks. First, I was in my second major depression, which was extremely painful for me and my loved ones. Just recently, when I asked my son Gabi, who is a neurologist and neurobiochemist, about that episode, he said, "I wished I could help you, felt scared of not knowing what was wrong, felt afraid I'd get depression knowing that your dad had committed suicide and here you were with the same problem...felt grateful after ECT because though sad, fragile, and frail, you were always more accessible and easier to connect with than just before you went into the hospital, felt grateful to have my brothers, felt grateful that 'Abba' (Hebrew for Dad) was as supportive and loving as a man can be." However, Georges said that despite the strong support of our children, he felt, "All alone in the world." So, this was a pretty shaky beginning to my Fourth Quarter.

Then, shortly after my recovery, boom: The COVID-19 pandemic hit. Whereas our labs came grinding to a halt, we were fortunate our kids were grown, and we no longer had any childcare responsibilities. This period was particularly difficult for young women, and some men, who needed to retreat from their careers to take care of their children and elders. That particularly affected women of limited means, especially women of color. However, even for well-to-do women, this was a difficult period. My daughter-in-law Mandy, who has an extremely supportive husband in David as a joint caregiver for her three children, went to work at the hospital without her usual peace of mind because rather than escaping from the responsibilities of the children's care while they were at school, now she needed to worry about what they were doing to occupy their minds and continue their learning rather than sit mindlessly staring at their iPads. The loss of school provided an opportunity for Georges and me, who would get onto Zoom and give the children science lessons. I taught them the molecular biology of coronavirus infection, including virus life cycles and the importance of RNA, and Georges taught them the physical principles of sanitizing with detergents and alcohols and how these disrupted the lipids in viral capsids. He also taught them the reasons for increased rainfall caused by global warming as well as the physical principles behind the warming of the planet.

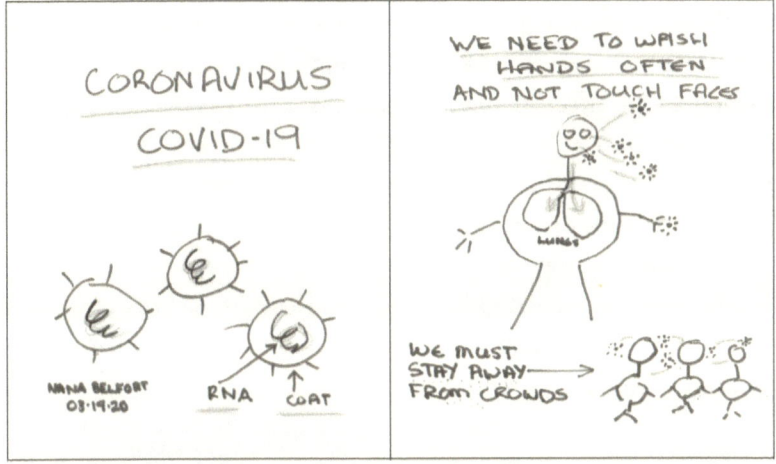

SLIDES FROM START OF PANDEMIC TO TEACH GRANCHILDREN, 2020: When we all went into lockdown at the very beginning of the pandemic, before schools started to teach remotely, Georges and I held sessions to teach our grandchildren science. These diagrams are from my class on COVID-19. **Left:** Structure of COVID-19 virus; **Right:** Human infection and sanitary practices.

A considerable aspect of the Fourth Quarter is looking back. We had a wonderful opportunity to do just that after the pandemic ended at the belated fiftieth anniversary symposium of Joan Steitz at Yale. Recall, Joan was a major female role model whom I introduced in Chapter Nine. From the slides, one could clearly time the advent of smartphones, when lab photos started to proliferate and DNA and then RNA sequencing was invented and big data appeared everywhere in the presentations. It was also marvelous to meet up with long-lost colleagues from the past, getting caught up and having a drink together as in years past. Then, there were the sad moments: those colleagues we lost along the way, Joan's husband Tom included. And, of couse, there were wrinkles where none existed before and thin, flabby skin beginning to replace the firm coatings of the past.

Wrinkles aside, ageism is inescapable and compounded by its intersectionality with other biases. Take for example the plumber and the gardener at the start of this chapter, when I asked about their being ageist or sexist or both. Did they look past me because I am a little old lady or merely because I'm a woman? Likewise, ageism intensifies the inequities of racism, amplifying the disadvantages and worsening the effects of both ageism and racism to the detriment of our communities. However, as our population has aged and the baby boomers navigate their seventies, there has been a slight uptick in cognizance of the problem, as reflected in Ageism Awareness Day and an emphasis on programs on healthy aging. There is hope.

One might argue all this talk of ageism is misplaced because ageism is actually different than all the other *-isms* in that it's universal; by definition, we *all* have a chance to be young and free of such bias. However, not everyone is old at the same time, so those of advanced age feel the discrimination in very real terms, be it at the gym, at the workplace, or speaking to the plumber. But then, we also sense the admiration of those who are impressed by our fortitude and resilience, and that restores the inner glow.

CHAPTER TWENTY-THREE

INTERGENERATIONAL INTERACTIONS

Intergenerational interactions are among the best ways to counter aging. As noted by Michelle Obama, "Spending time with children is the best antidote I've found to the challenges of facing injustice, fear or grief."[65] An NIH training grant in RNA science, on which I was co-principal investigator, keeps me in constant contact with my co-investigator, easily young enough to be my son, and a large cohort of the graduate students, who are just a few years older than my grandchildren. There's a wonderful reciprocity of learning, where they benefit from my research experience while I learn the modern ways of these future scientists. In general, university campuses lend themselves particularly well to intergenerational activities, as evident from the many retirement communities that are springing up near college campuses. The geographic proximity means the students can benefit from the wisdom and deep pockets of the elders, while the seniors are exposed to the campus's youthfulness as well as scientific

---

65 Obama, *The Light We Carry*.

and cultural activities that enrich their lives. In 2023, Paul Grondahl, the director of the esteemed NYS Writers Institute on the UAlbany campus, and I visited a senior living community, and he arranged for busloads of their citizens to visit the Book Fair and Film Festival on campus, where the seniors mingled with featured speakers and students alike. Lots of fun!

Georges recently took a trip to London with our three sons and nephew Marc Stern (Max's son) to celebrate Gabi's fiftieth birthday. They did what boys do: watched two English Premier League soccer games, ate, drank, told bad jokes, and roasted each other. By all accounts, they had a huge amount of fun. For us all, crossing the intergenerational divide keeps us young.

GUYS HAVING FUN IN LONDON, 2024: Gabi, Marc Stern (my brother Max's son), David, Georges and Yona outside a bar.

This brings me to our grandchildren, who provide a marvelous intergenerational focus to the Fourth Quarter. Zachary was the first of seven, born in 2005, when I was sixty. From when Zach was a baby, it was clear from the way he buckled the little belt in his high chair that he had inherited the scientist–engineering genes. On a different note, when he had just started talking, he looked at the jeans I was wearing, which had bold designs on them, and asked why I wear my pajamas in the daytime. I laughed out loud. Over the next ten years, when I entered the Fourth Quarter, we added Lincoln and Nadia, cousins born a month apart, Sequoia, Sam, Strand, and Levi. Five reside in the Boston area, two in Cape Elizabeth, in southern Maine, and despite the distance and the decade that separates them, they love each other dearly and relish being together, to say nothing about how much Georges and I enjoy them, both individually and collectively. I learn so much from them. Zach, Linc, and Nadia help us negotiate our electronic devices. Linc and I talk politics, and he teaches me about the business of high fashion. He and I love to knit together, teach each other new stitches, and compare patterns. And Nadia, my ladybug, has taught me what it's like to have a little girl among us after three sons and two grandsons. Nadia used to sleep in the walk-in closet off Georges's and my bedroom at the Cape house and stood next to my bed one morning, quite indignant, asking, "Nana, why do you hang your clothes in my bedroom?" How beautiful to see the world through the eyes of children!

Lincoln and Nadia, first cousins, are tight friends, as are Nadia and Sequoia, the only two girls. Quoi, as we call her, is fascinated by science, and she and cousin Zach will frequently ask questions about the physical universe and biological principles. Quoi, who really resonates with the scientist in me, asked me one day if I'm famous. I told her, "A teeny bit." Then there are the cousins Sam and Strand, born a half year apart, who often spend time together with us as they discuss the history of Maine and whether they will surf or play soccer or basketball. The littlest of the bunch, Levi, is totally fascinated by marine biology and brings back bucketsful of clams, oysters, and mussels from the beach for his inspection and eventual cooking and eating. All the children have taken pottery lessons in various combinations near our home on the Cape. I have lots of little pots and bowls of theirs, receptacles for sauces and half-used tea bags. Next year, I plan to attend pottery classes along with them rather than simply dropping them off. Growing together brings us all joy.

SEVEN GRANDCHILDREN, 2016: Our seven grandchildren are the apples of our eyes and help keep me and Georges young in our Fourth Quarter of life. Baby Levi is in the stroller and the others, **L to R**, are Sam, Strand, Nadia, Zachary, Lincoln, and Sequoia. Here they are on a neighborhood beach near our home in North Falmouth on Cape Cod.

We also like to discuss social activism with the grandkids, and at Thanksgiving, they each pick a charity, and Georges and I make small donations in their names. Their selections range from animal care to the environment and disaster relief to feeding the hungry. It's important for children of privilege to think of those less fortunate.

All seven grandchildren enjoy math and science, some are gifted artists, others are history and politics buffs. All are physically active in everything from soccer and lacrosse to ice hockey, surfing, rock climbing, tennis, and gymnastics. We sometimes work out together on Saturday mornings. Our children and grandchildren display their relative nimbleness while Georges and I show how one can enjoy moving even if in a more limited fashion. Family gatherings over Thanksgiving, the Fourth of July, birthdays, and the Jewish holidays are also favorites, and we all pitch in with our favorite dishes to make these feasts happen. The family events are always festive and noisy, where it's sometimes hard to get a word in, and of course, that's rough when everyone's bursting with strong opinions.

Several of the children love to cook, as do I, and we do everything from baking muffins to rolling matzo balls. Watching soccer together, be it the English Premier League or the US men or women in the World Cup, is also a favorite activity. During the COVID-19 pandemic, our get-togethers were more limited, but in early 2023, as restrictions were lifted, Georges and I, our three sons, our three daughters-in-law, and our seven grandchildren, fifteen in total, took a trip to South Africa together.

We visited Cape Town, one of the iconic cities of the world, and Simbavati, a game reserve, where we saw four of the "big five" animals: lion, rhino, elephant, and buffalo. Despite not seeing a leopard, the fifth, this was a very exciting shared experience. Cape Town was the high point due to its beauty and all the family history: It was, of course, the town in which Georges and I grew up, fell in love, and married. It was also where some of the kids' ancestors lived and were buried. The children surfed the waves of the Indian Ocean, enjoyed the beaches of the Atlantic, and were taken in by the awe-inspiring views from Table Mountain. They met our childhood friends, who remarked on how much our granddaughters, Nadia and Sequoia, reminded them of me at the same age. The girls loved hearing that, as did I. I felt proud, and the comments transported me back to my lively teenage years. We also visited with my brother Max and his lovely wife, Rene. They also immigrated to the US (California) in the mid-1970s but returned to South Africa in 2020 to be with Renee's sisters. They have two children in California whom we feel close to, and this allows us to see the Sterns on annual visits to the West coast.

Our children also loved seeing our alma mater, the University of Cape Town, from which Georges and I graduated in the mid-1960s and received honorary doctorates in 2019. Both Georges and I had been invited to sign UCT's Golden Book, which is a record of visiting dignitaries to UCT who have been granted honorary degrees. That was a truly humbling experience, signing pages in the same book as luminaries like Bill Clinton, Nelson Mandela, Barack Obama, and Desmond Tutu. The children marveled at those signatures. They were also captivated by Mandela's modest prison cell on Robben Island, where he spent the first eighteen of his twenty-seven years in confinement.

HANGING OUT IN THE WILD, SIMBAVATI LODGE, SOUTH AFRICA, 2023: We took an extraordinary trip to South Africa with our whole family: Georges and I, our three sons, our three daughters-in-law, and our seven grandchildren. Here, fourteen of us are having a "Sundowner" drink—the fifteenth is asleep in the Jeep.

WITH THE GOLDEN BOOK, 2023: On our family trip to South Africa, we viewed UCT's Golden Book, a record of visiting dignitaries who have received honorary degrees, including ourselves. It was surreal to see our signatures alongside such luminaries as Bill Clinton, Nelson Mandela, Barak Obama, and Desmond Tutu. **Left bottom:** Cover of the Golden Book. **Left top:** Nelson Mandela's page with signature from 1990. **Right:** Georges and I with my page and signature from 2019.

All three of our sons and two of their wives, Erin and Mandy, had visited South Africa before, but for Sara and the grandchildren, this was a first. Everyone was enthralled. They enjoyed the food, fished from the Cape waters and grown on the fertile land under brilliant sunshine. But they were also aware of a political unraveling taking place in the country. After Mandela was released from prison in 1990, the country moved to abandon Apartheid and establish a democratic government in 1994 under his presidency. Until 1999, when Mandela left office, South Africa thrived and was a place of optimism and great hope as the "rainbow nation." But since then, the country has suffered from enormous corruption, broken promises, and dismantled services, including the postal service, train system, and even the electricity grid. There is also widespread fear of theft, carjacking, and violence. We therefore needed to be careful to confine ourselves to spaces known to be safe.

There was no avoiding the busy Cape Town waterfront surrounding the docks. Though bustling with activity—the waterfront is popular with everyone and seen as the one last vestige of a rainbow nation—it is also the place my father was found drowned in his car more than six decades earlier. But the sadness I felt was woven into a kind of fabric with the children's threads of curiosity and joyfulness. I tried to identify and tease out the disparate emotions running through me. Might I have felt the presence of my dad in that moment and how he was pleased to have his grandchildren and great-grandchildren there with his daughter? Or was I noticing my own pleasure and gratitude toward my offspring for helping me overcome the pain my dad had inflicted on me with his suicide?

We also took the whole family, all fifteen of us, to my childhood home in Oranjezicht overlooking the Atlantic Ocean and to the Jewish cemetery in Pinelands, where both Georges's and my parents are buried. I was dreading the cemetery and went there—along with our children and grandchildren—with a heavy heart. A feeling of trepidation and sadness hung over me. But as the entire family hovered over the graves of our parents, grandparents, and great-grandparents, the children hugged and held Georges and me, and my dread transformed into a deep sense of fulfillment and pride. The children's emotions were palpable; they were clearly moved. Interestingly, after leaving South Africa, we collectively analyzed our travels around Cape Town and Simbavati game reserve, with the children recalling all their favorite places and animals, and the older grandkids concluded the visit to the Pinelands cemetery was the most evocative and meaningful part of the trip for them. Two months later, when we were all at Sequoia's Bat Mitzvah in Boston, she handed me a stone that she had picked up from my mother's grave site and saved for me. We were standing in front of a table draped with a cloth intricately embroidered by Oma, my grandmother and Quoi's great-great-grandmother. A span of five generations represented in one spot. It hardly gets any better than that.

Being with Nadia and Sequoia is a special experience for me, having raised only boys. They and their mothers are the daughters I never had. Sometimes, we just have fun doing the frivolous things girls like to do, like painting our fingernails, going for pedicures, or shopping for clothes. And sometimes, we have deeply important conversations, like the status of women in different cultures and how important it is for women to be in control of their lives, bodies, and reproductive choices. There are also intimate adult discussions, like a conversation about contraception where one daughter-in-law confessed to her intrauterine device having fallen out, the second to feeling impatient about conceiving, and the third to being pregnant with her third child.

WITH DAUGHTERS-IN-LAW, 2018: My three daughters-in-law—Sara, Erin, and Mandy **(L to R)**—are very dear to me, and how crazy is it that all three are pediatricians? Hence, the title of the book, asked by one of our grandchildren, "Mommy, can boys also be doctors?"

We also have our separate relationships. David's wife Mandy and I bond over scholarship, given that in addition to her clinical responsibilities as a neonatologist at Brigham and Women's Hospital, she is an NIH-funded researcher at Harvard Medical School. We laugh when our scientific papers are sometimes misattributed since we're both M. B. Belfort and lament about the difficulties of academic life. Gabi's wife Sara, "the *real* pediatrician," and I bemoan the hardships in medical practice today, where she sees a patient every twenty minutes at one of Mass General Brigham's outpatient pediatric clinics. Imagine the impossibility of treating a fourteen-year-old patient who comes into the clinic complaining of nausea and fatigue, is given a pregnancy diagnosis, and needs counseling and coordination of care all in twenty minutes! Thankfully, Sara has a new job in a small nonprofit pediatric practice where she gets to spend a full thirty minutes with each child. Then there is Yona's wife, Erin, a child psychiatrist at Maine Medical Center and in private practice. One of her specialties is treating gender diverse and transgender youth and their families. We talk about how sad it is that the identity of these adolescents is threatened and their access to healthcare is under attack. Erin also likes to write and often shares her work for me to edit. Also, Erin has started a professional woman's group, which I'm told was indirectly influenced by me. Although sometimes I feel like I may overstep my bounds with my daughters-in-law, or that they may underreach, we're basically a cohesive bunch with a great deal of mutual respect, admiration, and love.

It's pretty amazing that all three of our sons married pediatricians, albeit of different flavors. Also remarkable is that these women did not know each other before they joined our family. They all get along well, and I'm often amused by their counseling one another and each other's families according to their different subspecialties. Although boys *can* also be doctors, these three women are extraordinary!

As one might imagine, there's rarely a lull in the conversation, even if it's me reassuring them that life will get simpler. They're interested to know why I claim that older is easier. I tell them it's not only because of the children making their own way but also because of the passing of debilitating perfectionism—most things seem good enough now. Also, the need to keep striving is over. Whereas the entire family helps me age with purpose, I help the next generation, and the next as well, by showing them aging can be cool and not something to be dreaded.

CHAPTER TWENTY-FOUR

PASSING THE BATON

While my generation is enjoying our retirement and leisure time, many of us also feel the need to hand down to future generations such imperatives as the importance of caring for our planet, civil rights, and social justice, as well as respect for the truth. Needless to say, all of these values have been seriously tested over the past decade, especially after Donald Trump won the 2016 election, defeating Hillary Clinton. Although he lost the popular vote, the electoral college went his way. That same year, the British voted in favor of Brexit, to leave the European Union. That was a disastrous beginning to my Fourth Quarter. I, like most of my fellow scientists, am a truth junky.[66] Our work involves boring for the truth. Consider our despair at learning that the *Oxford Dictionary*'s 2016 word of the year was "post-truth," which implies that objective facts are less important than personal belief or political agenda. The Brexit referendum and US presidential election popularized the word but left scientists like us demoralized because our currency—facts—was being devalued and undermined

---

66 Marlene Belfort, "Science as Tranquilizer and Trailblazer," BioMed Central, January 30, 2017, https://blogs.biomedcentral.com/bmcblog/2017/01/30/science-as-tranquilizer-and-trailblazer/.

before our very eyes. Whereas "alternative truths" drift and change, real truths are fixed and need to form the foundation for our future.

It gets worse than that. Entire academic value systems are under siege. In conservative states like Florida, Texas, and even Ohio, it is illegal to teach the history of slavery—the facts. Diversity initiatives are being stymied, and politicians, rather than academics, are taking over at the helms of universities in conservative states, in part to facilitate the bending of the truth. There are also conservative activists attempting to undermine universities by targeting affirmative action, and in 2023, the US Supreme Court actually *ruled* against affirmative action to limit the use of racial identity in college admissions. Scientists need to be part of the resistance that stands up for the truth and affirmative action, the force that bores for facts individually, collectively, and globally, adding to the knowledge base that will carry us forward.

An example of scientists successfully trumpeting the truth is during the COVID-19 pandemic, where the mRNA vaccine, based on decades of thorough and sound fundamental scientific research, triumphed over the nonsense of drinking bleach and saved tens of millions of lives, as described aptly in books by Tom Cech and Tony Fauci, the former director of the National Institute of Allergy and Infectious Diseases.[67] Continuing to perform research of the highest quality and lobbying for continued investment in the research enterprise by our federal funding agencies are paramount. I will do battle for the truth until my dying day.

The healing power of truth is perhaps best exemplified by Archbishop Desmond Tutu, whom I quoted at the start of Part Four and who presided over the Truth and Reconciliation Commission in South Africa, set up in 1995 by Nelson Mandela's government after his peaceful rise to power at the beginning of the post-Apartheid era. Tutu's Commission was like a court, designed to help ease the country's pain by revealing the truth about the atrocities and human rights

---

67   Cech, *The Catalyst*; Anthony Fauci, *On Call: A Doctor's Journey in Public Service* (Viking, 2024).

violations of the Apartheid era. The focus of the court was to dig up the truth about both the perpetrators of injustice and violence and the victims of these crimes. Reconciliation was achieved merely by exposing the truth and abandoning the cover-ups and the lies. No prosecutions, no arrests, only truth! Perhaps we could use a Truth and Reconciliation Commission here in the United States to help us bridge the political divide?

Lying also just seems to me a burdensome way to live. Although the truth may be taxing at the start, it is surely less arduous in the long run. But bereft scientists can't do it alone; other lovers of our planet must mobilize against lies and the many other horrors that face us today. There is global warming in the face of climate skepticism, described as a Chinese hoax, invented, it is argued, to damage US global competitiveness. More pure nonsense! There is racism, anti-Semitism, Islamophobia, and homophobia. There is the loss of women's reproductive choices, rising economic disparities, and gun violence. There is food insecurity, infectious disease outbreaks, and the rise of global antimicrobial-drug resistance. There is unregulated AI. Scientists can lead the charge on many of these fronts, but we also need to spread the message in a digestible form to society in general and our children in particular. We need to restore public trust in scholarship and make our children understand the value of science, which provides the best basis to prevent and cure disease, purify water, and grow food, to invent for a bright economic future and help save the planet from lies.

It was therefore with much delight that I read in the *New York Times* in 2022 of an idealistic young Rhodes Scholar named Jaz Brisack, a general studies major working as a barista at a Starbucks in Buffalo, New York.[68] She took this job to initiate efforts to unionize the store and indeed the chain. She has since moved on to Tesla and written a book titled *Get on the Job and Organize* about the creation of

---

68 Noam Scheiber, "Why a Rhodes Scholar's Ambition Led Her to a Job at Starbucks," *New York Time*, June 19, 2022, https://www.nytimes.com/2022/06/19/business/starbucks-union-rhodes-scholar.html.

a new labor movement.⁶⁹ Her unionization success, right after graduating from Oxford University, stimulated in me two trains of thought. One was the student activism of the late 1960s that turned public opinion against the Vietnam War and eventually led to the reduction of troops and elimination of the draft. We formed a counterculture that resisted, cultivated the women's movement, and fought for civil rights. The passion of youth drove change. Which brings me to my second thought, which was about the voices of our young people today. Are they loud enough? Are they doing enough to carry the torch? Peaceful protest movements on campuses in favor of peace in the Middle East are a step in the right direction, regardless of the pain they cause me. One can only hope the strong pro-Palestine and pro-Israel protests that have been ongoing since the outbreak of the Hamas–Israel war on October 7, 2023, will reach some common understanding of each other's pain as a path to peace.

I feel particularly unsettled by the recent campus protests and encampments not only because of my sensitivity to both anti-Semitism and Islamophobia and having lived in Israel but also because exercising free speech is an important right of which we were deprived as the children of Apartheid South Africa. Also, diversity and inclusivity are important principles of mine. In a recent *New York Times* editorial, "Universities Are Failing at Inclusion," David Brooks made the point that universities need to be fostering tolerance of different views and backgrounds rather than being ideological battlefields.⁷⁰ Brooks proposed that offended donors, rather than withdrawing funds from universities, should invest in creating institutes that focus on promoting mutual understanding and cooperation. While in favor of peaceful protest to effect change, I strongly agree that we need to be paying closer attention to what unites us rather than what tears us apart.

---

69 Jaz Brisack, *Get on the Job and Organize: The Making of a New Labor Movement* (Atria/One Signal, 2025).

70 David Brooks, "Universities Are Failing at Inclusion," *New York Times*, opinion, November 16, 2023, https://www.nytimes.com/2023/11/16/opinion/college-university-antisemitism-crt.html.

There have been a few other important protest movements started in the last twenty years, one of the most visible being on behalf of education for girls in Muslim countries led by Malala Yousafzai. Malala was shot by the Taliban because of her fight for the cause of female education in Pakistan and was awarded the Nobel Peace prize for her work at the tender age of seventeen. Then, another young woman, Greta Thunberg, the Swedish environmental activist, at age fifteen began a global charge against climate change. And there's X (Emma) González, the activist who survived the Stoneman Douglas High School shooting in Parkland, Florida, and went on a gun-control crusade, founding the advocacy group Never Again MSD and organizing the historic March for Our Lives. This uprising coincided with the #MeToo movement, which was in response to sexual harassment and triggered by the high-profile cases of abusive men such as film producer Harvey Weinstein and President Donald Trump. It gives me a degree of satisfaction to note that all these dissenters are young women.

A notable protest that was more male dominated was Occupy Wall Street, a populist movement that protested in the financial district of New York City against economic imbalance and corporate greed, but the interest group fizzled after just a couple months. The Black Lives Matter movement, ignited by the deaths of black men such as George Floyd at the hands of white police officers, has been longer lived, geographically more diverse, and involving people of all races, genders, and ages to highlight racism and police violence against black people. The movement persists, regrettably alongside the unabating problem of police brutality. There are also many long-lived LGBTQ+ movements rallying support for gay, lesbian, bisexual, transgender, and queer folks, leading to greater acceptance in a growing number of countries worldwide. Despite the remaining illegality of gender nonconformity in some nations, many countries have now legalized same-sex marriage.

I am encouraged too by how our youth stood up recently to save the environment in Montana. There were sixteen young plaintiffs of mixed genders, all under the age of twenty-two, who sued their conservative state for violating their constitutional rights to a healthy environment in support of environmental groups that are challenging the permit for a gas pipeline along the Yellowstone River.[71] Of course, the hope is their victory will be a precedent-setting action for other states.

But how about abortion? And the threat to our democracy? It is well documented that the younger age demographic is predominantly pro-choice and politically progressive. In the spirit of Greta Thunberg, Jaz Brisack, and the Montana sixteen, I am relying on our youth to organize and get these major jobs done. My appeal to the young folks is to stand up and change the world, to vote to save our futures, to take seriously the often-paraphrased sentiments of Dr. Martin Luther King, Jr., "Our lives begin to end the day we become silent about things that matter."[72] It is the young folks who need to help make our world a more hospitable place for us all, and particularly for themselves and their offspring.

---

[71] David Gelles and Mike Baker, "Judge Rules in Favor of Montana Youths in a Landmark Climate Case," *New York Times*, August 14, 2023, https://www.nytimes.com/2023/08/14/us/montana-youth-climate-ruling.html.

[72] Paraphrase of Martin Luther King Jr., sermon, Selma, Alabama, March 8, 1965.

AFTERWORD

APPROACHING THE FINISH LINE

"It's not over till it's over."

—Yogi Berra

"I cannot pretend I am without fear. But my predominant feeling is one of gratitude. I have loved and been loved; I have been given much and I have given something in return; I have read and traveled and thought and written. I have had an intercourse with the world…"

—Oliver Sacks, *Gratitude*

My recent public talks have allowed for retrospection, looking back at my research and the integration of my scientific career with the other facets of my life. Those other facets include my family, of course, and various setbacks and illnesses along my sometimes-haphazard journey filled with both trauma and triumph. From their feedback, I sense these talks release some of the tension within young scientists in the audience, who appear to feel constrained in their responses to all their callings and passions. I remember an email I received back in 2003 when I published the article on "Microbiological Moms."[73] "I picked up your article at the 103rd meeting of ASM in Washington, DC. I've recently made a decision to go back to school to get my PhD in microbiology. I have two daughters, aged eight and five. Before I read your article, I was really feeling guilty about my decision. Your article has put things in perspective for me. Having another mother articulate what I'm going through has made a difference. Thank you." It's important for me to reveal to my audiences and my readers my vulnerabilities along with my strengths, for their sake as well as for mine.

Here are some of the life lessons I hope have emerged from this book and may be reassuring or even useful to you, the reader:

- Muddling through is okay. When you grope and probe and poke and bumble and bungle, you eventually find the switch and see the light.
- When bad things happen to us, as they inevitably do in life, we must pick ourselves up, and that builds resilience. Likewise, when we fear we've done terrible things to our children despite a loving environment, we must remind ourselves that our failures can be a true gift to our children because they teach *them* to bounce back from the adversities *they* are bound to encounter in *their* lives.
- Living the truth is easier than living lies and holds up in the long run.
- It's very rewarding to capitalize on our good fortune by paying it forward.
- It's okay to follow rules when you need to and to break them when you can. Said differently, it's prudent to walk the line between caution and boldness.
- Magic often happens at the fringes.
- Going against the grain of conventional wisdom is okay too.
- It's good to walk toward those who can help us and who love us and to have the courage to walk away from those who don't.

---

73   Belfort, "Microbiological Moms, Their Sisters and Brothers."

- The best we can hope for our children is that they are healthy and happy.
- None of us is perfect, but most of us are good enough.
- In the words of my mom, "Each loss is an opportunity."
- And in *my* words, "Letting go is liberating."

But remember, these are not intended as formal advice, which, as I said at the start of the book, I hesitate to give. Each of us has our own story, our personal narrative. These are simply the insights that came out of mine, the lessons I've learned over the course of a long, bumpy, and fulfilled life.

And now, as I look back and glimpse forward, I think about Erik Erikson's stages of psychosocial development. The final, or eighth, stage is focused on old age, as we reflect on the life we've lived. Will we leave our journey on earth feeling satisfied or remorseful, fulfilled or despairing? I came into this life wanting to be a mom, and I will leave as one, with no regrets of not having nursed my children long enough or having given them less than what I could squeeze out for them. In fact, more than ever, the mom role feels like the pillar in me. But as I approach eighty, I also find, reciprocally, that the children support me as I navigate my Fourth Quarter.

As for the scientist in me, I look back at my career, filled with success way beyond my wildest dreams, and I'm most grateful for that. Grateful for the new knowledge we unearthed and the molecular understanding we gained of a tiny facet of life; grateful for the thrill of surprise findings and the brilliant students who made those discoveries; grateful for the opportunities to travel, to meet the best and the brightest; and grateful for the recognition and respect of my fellow scientists and nonscientists alike. However, my career accomplishments fall far behind the satisfaction I get from being an attentive mom, an adoring daughter, a loving wife, a nourishing sister, a cool grandma, a warm in-law, a caring aunt, a loyal friend, and a supportive colleague. I have much more nurturing yet to do, and when I'm done, by Erikson's criteria, I will be at peace with a life well lived, well loved, and richly textured.

ACKNOWLEDGMENTS

The writing of this book was stimulated by multitudes of uncertain young people who have crossed my path over decades, and was encouraged by my niece Lisa Bernard, a news journalist, to whom I dared show the nascent first draft. She provided the impetus to continue writing and to publish. Then, there is my friend and colleague Paul Grondahl, the director of the New York State (NYS) Writers Institute, who felt I had a story to tell. When I had a kernel of a book, there came along Mark Chait, my editor, the son of a childhood friend, whose input was critical by asking all the right questions and making superb suggestions. Mark's kindness and thoughtfulness were important to building my confidence as a novice in this new genre of nonscience writing. Mark was ever-patient, caring, smart, insightful, honest, appreciative, and instrumental in my making it across the finish line. I also thank Mark's colleagues at Scribe Media for their editing services, and particularly Ellie Cole for her expert guidance, attention to detail, and kindness, as well Anna Dorfman for her creative rendering of the cover of the book. And Mark's dad, Alan Chait, my childhood friend and talented photographer, helped refine some of the pictures.

Friends and colleagues provided invaluable input by reading drafts at various stages and sharing memories. My literary friends, George and Sharon Gmelch, Kathy Zdeb, Helen McComas, Sandra Chait, and Judy Frangos egged me on. My scientific friends and colleagues, Arlene Ramsingh, Elga Wulfert, Nancy Craig, Paolo Forni, and Shekhar Garde identified soft spots in the narrative and helped me firm them up. Tom Cech, John Inglis, and Pamela Rothstein provided encouragement during the final stages of the manuscript based on their experience in book publishing. And then there are those other friends and colleagues, too numerous to mention, who have travelled along with me on my life's journey, sturdied me, loved me along the way, and provided the opportunity for me to enrich *their* lives.

My students and post-docs were my inspiration and my partners in discovery. They taught me much and kept me buoyed by their curiosity and providing interesting experimental results. My technicians and lab managers, with a special shout-out to Carol Lyn Piazza, Dorie Smith, and Matt Stanger, kept me grounded and organized, and together, the members of this lab family were my partners in science. They provided not only the support but also the data on which my career was based.

The support and wisdom of my psychiatrist, Gregory Lavigne, who understood me, treated me, and provided therapy from mid-life into my golden years, were critical to my regaining and maintaining my sanity. Our cousin Jack Hirschowitz, also a psychiatrist, offered useful insights and reassurances during critical downtimes. And then, the women in Group, WISH and WoW, whether therapists or regular humans, gave the support, appreciation, and friendship that steadied me throughout.

My extended family was always there for me and gave me support when I most needed it. They include my brother Max; his amazing wife Rene; their son Marc; my equally amazing sister-in-law Ethel; my brothers-in-law David, Hilton, and Lindsay; my cousins Gerd, Renee, and their families; and my other cousins, nieces, and nephews. Also, Georges's French family and the Rabbi's clan in Israel jointly make me feel like a citizen of the world.

Most importantly, my nuclear family gave me the love and the lived experience that anchored the content of this book. They also gave important feedback on the narrative. The inner circle includes Georges, my lover, life's partner, friend, and advocate, the father of my children, David, Gabi, and Yona. The four of them are the collective wind behind my sails; it's as if they keep me breathing through constant contact and sharing the nuances of our lives. They help piece me together when I fall apart and make me feel like the luckiest woman on this earth when I'm whole again. Then, my wonderful and impressive daughters-in-law, Mandy, Sara, and Erin, who balance, juggle, and do important work in their communities as they infuse our family with kindness, love, and wisdom and make me feel my value as a mother-in-law. And *their* children, my grandchildren, the loves of my life, Zachary, Lincoln, Nadia, Sequoia, Sam, Strand, and Levi. Watching them grow from those first ultrasound images through infancy into childhood, teenhood, and now young adulthood has been the privilege of a lifetime, a profound thrill, and source of huge pride.

Finally, my late father taught me resilience the hard way, while my late mother, Oma, and Bessie taught me about strong women and nurtured in me the confidence to become a committed mom and self-reliant scientist.

Thank you, all!

ABOUT THE AUTHOR

DR. MARLENE BELFORT was born in South Africa to German-Jewish refugees escaping Hitler's regime. One of the first women to study graduate biochemistry and microbiology at the University of Cape Town, she earned her PhD from the University of California, Irvine, and conducted postdoctoral research at the Hebrew University, Jerusalem, and Northwestern University. A member of the US National Academy of Sciences and a Fellow of the American Academy of Arts and Sciences, she holds the International RNA Society's Lifetime Achievement Award. Dr. Belfort is a Distinguished Professor at SUNY at Albany. She and her husband, Georges, live in Massachusetts.

www.ingramcontent.com/pod-product-compliance
Lightning Source LLC
Chambersburg PA
CBHW030442090526
44586CB00044B/552